*Perspectives For Living* is based on two series for BBC Radio 4 in which Bel Mooney interviews twelve people about the way one particular death affected their lives. Each interview concentrates on a different loss, but the effect is to remind us most powerfully that loss is both unique and universal. What the interviews have in common is an understanding of gain through loss. It might represent (as in the case of Lord Hailsham) an intensification of religious faith; or (as with Clare Short) a simple, humanistic faith in the perpetual nature of human goodness. But all twelve people have truly achieved a perspective for living – a knowledge that loss places you permanently on the interface between suffering and acceptance, and that grief and love are two sides of the same coin.

Chris Patten talks about his mother, and Dan Topolski about his father. Bernard Levin remembers the loss of a dear friend, and biographer Anne Chisholm describes the tragic early death of her sister – which, with sad irony, provided her with an unexpected gift. Clare Short honours the memory of a happy childhood of which her father Frank was the centre. The novelist Alice Thomas Ellis, actor Barrie Rutter, and Val Hazel all tell of the particularly painful experience of losing a child, whilst Lord Hailsham and the poet Pamela Gillilan talk about the death of a beloved spouse. Equally moving is Tony Whitehead's description of the deterioration, through AIDS, of his partner; and Christopher Booker's haunting story of the murder of his younger sister.

**Bel Mooney** is the author of fourteen books, many of them for children. She has also made a name as an interviewer of great sensitivity on Channel 4, BBC 2 and Radio 4. In 1984 she was presented with an award by the Queen, as President of the charity CRUSE, for her articles on bereavement in the national press. When not in London, she lives just outside Bath.

D0756398

*All manner of thing shall be well*
  *When the tongues of flame are in-folded*
  *Into the crowned knot of fire*
  *And the fire and the rose are one.*

T.S. Eliot, 'Little Gidding'

# PERSPECTIVES FOR LIVING

*Conversations on Bereavement
and Love*

## Bel Mooney

With photographs by Robin Allison Smith

JOHN MURRAY

First published in 1992
by John Murray (Publishers) Ltd.,
50 Albemarle Street, London W1X 4BD

A catalogue record for this book is available from the British Library

ISBN 0–7195–5125 0

Typeset in 11.5/13.5 Garamond 3 by
Wearset, Boldon, Tyne and Wear
Printed and bound in Great Britain by
Butler & Tanner Ltd., Frome and London

In memory of Peter Jenkins
(1934–1992)


*Still are thy pleasant voices, thy nightingales awake;*
*For Death, he taketh all away, but them he cannot take.*

W. Cory, 'Heraclitus'

# Contents

*Introduction* 1

*Author's Note* 11

1 CHRISTOPHER BOOKER · *sister* 15

2 ANNE CHISHOLM · *sister* 33

3 PAMELA GILLILAN · *husband* 47

4 LORD HAILSHAM · *wife* 63

5 ANNA HAYCRAFT · *grown-up son* 81

6 VAL HAZEL · *son* 97

7 BERNARD LEVIN · *friend* 113

8 CHRIS PATTEN · *mother* 127

9 BARRIE RUTTER · *baby son* 139

10 CLARE SHORT · *father* 153

11 DANIEL TOPOLSKI · *father* 171

# CONTENTS

12  TONY WHITEHEAD · *lover*                187

*Appendix*                                   203

*Suggested Reading*                          214

# INTRODUCTION

*What man shall live and not see death?*
Psalms 89:49

Throughout the ages, in all cultures, the living have been preoccupied with death: fearing it, facing it, wondering what lies beyond it. The struggle to stay alive is common to animals and to man, and yet only the human race is given the ability to face death consciously, and perhaps with the equanimity which reflects the highest qualities of a life led well. The ceremonials of death are the most significant in any society, because they reflect the value placed on life by that people, as well as their conception of meaning and of destiny. As the literatures of the world reveal, death is the object of reflection in moments of introspection, and of most solemn ritual. In *Beowulf*, when Scyld's body is cast out on the waters in a boat fitted out for a long journey, the anonymous author of the great Anglo-Saxon poem comments that no man, no matter how powerful or influential, can know 'who unloaded that boat'. In poetry, drama, fiction and philosophy, love and death are the two greatest themes.

In twentieth-century popular culture, death has always found a role in the creations of scriptwriters – from the brutality of airborne warfare to the sentimentality of *Love Story*, with many a murder in between. Yet few have addressed themselves to grief itself, and (perhaps more important) to the idea of life after death. It was interesting therefore, that the period in between the

1

recording of each series of *A Perspective for Living* for BBC Radio 4 saw the release of two films, one British, one American, bold enough to address the issue, and with some humour too. Although the British *Truly, Madly, Deeply*, and the American *Ghost* are very different, they share one message at least: that love and grief are two sides of the same coin. They acknowledge this truth – that although the beloved dead may never really leave us, we have to experience both love and grief in order to be released into living on without them.

*Truly, Madly, Deeply* is the story of one woman's inability to come to terms with grief for her dead lover. The acute (therapists might call it 'hysterical') grief is externalized, and the ghost of the man comes back in material form to live with her once more. This extra time together mirrors the real time: sometimes ecstatic, sometimes irritable – although in her grief she had grown to idealize the relationship, and forgotten how selfish and demanding her lover could be. This curiously corporeal ghost complains of being permanently chilly, and eventually invites spirit-friends back (absurdly) to watch videos. Understandably, she objects to her flat being full of intrusive 'dead people'. In the meantime she has met someone else, whom she recognizes, instinctively, as her future partner – but this will only happen when she has been able to let go of her ghost (her grief), and he of her. At the end of the film, movingly, he watches at the window with the other spirits as she walks down the path to be with her new man.

*Ghost* has a different emphasis. When the hero is murdered we meet his shade immediately; all people, it seems, carry their spirit within them, released at the moment of death into the realm of light, or else dragged by dark shadows to damnation. A medieval fresco artist, working on a vision of 'The Last Judgement' in any church across Europe, would have had no difficulty with this iconography-in-motion. In *Ghost* it is the spirit himself, and his mission to protect his girlfriend, which is central; her grief, though real, is incidental. The film is about an unquiet spirit who, seeking just retribution and acting as a protector to the living, can, when his task is completed, be rewarded with heavenly bliss. This is, one might say, a classic 'literary' ghost, whilst the British film is about a 'psychological' ghost; and perhaps the success of both indicates that the modern audience, deprived of the opportunity to contemplate such things, has a profound need for the consolation to be found in both films.

Some form of consolation was, I hope, one of the effects of the two Radio 4 series of interviews, *A Perspective For Living*, that make up this book – consolation both for those interviewed and for listeners and readers. That was certainly one intention. Another was to assert that it is neither depressing nor morbid to talk about death. As Anna Haycraft (the novelist Alice Thomas Ellis) replied when I wrote to ask her to participate: 'What else is there to talk about?'

It is now a cliché to say that death has become the great taboo, and the truth of it can even be questioned. Certainly Geoffrey Gorer was right in identifying the modern inhibition; in his pioneering 1956 essay, 'The Pornography of Death', he pointed out that for his generation, sex could be talked about but death could not. We may look back at the excesses of the nineteenth century – the yards of black crêpe, the hair plaited into rings and brooches, the atrophied diction of mourning verse – and rejoice that the pompous, melancholy cortège has trundled into the shadows forever. Yet there might be a case to argue that in the last ten years or so, far from being a taboo, death has become a fashionable subject. There are many books on the management of grief; if a tragedy afflicts a small town in America nowadays, the place is promptly invaded by bereavement counsellors and therapists. This may, or may not be a good thing. My point, though, is that the books and the counsellors do little to replace death at the philosophical centre stage. They still treat grief like a sickness, needing careful treatment, or an aberration which must be managed. In Philippe Aries's terms, we have moved, since the Middle Ages, from a 'Tamed Death' – accepted absolutely and prepared for – to a 'Forbidden Death' – shoved to one side so that the bland course of life is barely disturbed. If you must scream out the pain of loss you must do it very quietly, so the neighbours will not be upset.

Since childhood I have loved graveyards, especially country churchyards, not merely because they are places of peace, nor for the beauty of the lettering on eighteenth-century tombs, but simply because, in Larkin's phrase, 'so many dead lie around'. Such places are full of spirits: the nineteenth-century parents who outlived their eight children demand sympathy still, as do the young men listed on the war memorials who were sent to be slaughtered. The names, the symbolism of broken column and winged cherub, the awkwardly rhyming epitaphs and platitudes of faith are all reminders of mortality, allowing the dead to teach the living, as they ought. Most telling of all, for me, are the *memento mori*, the skulls carved in stone and slate which were a popular symbol until the nineteenth century. There are grinning ones, and odd geometric ones, and ones with crossed bones, and full-length skeletons – and they have two functions. The first is, of course, to instil terror. This is Hamlet, holding Yorick's skull: 'Now get you to my lady's chamber and tell her, let her paint an inch thick, to this favour she must come . . .'. *Vanitas vanitorum* – the skull is the terrible warning of what fate awaits us all, fear and horror the only response.

Yet there is another interpretation, one linked to the vivid sugar skulls Mexican children are bought to celebrate The Day of the Dead, and the little skeleton toys they play with. This moves beyond fear to an acceptance of the inevitability of death, as well as the permanence of the spirit. A Mexican peasant family would understand the films *Ghost* and *Truly, Madly, Deeply*; each year, on All Souls Night, they set a place at the table for their beloved dead, knowing that they return to visit, and that they want the living to celebrate, not to grieve. In the words of Octavio Paz, 'The word death is not pronounced in New York, in Paris, in London, because it burns the lips. The Mexican, in contrast, is familiar with death, jokes about it, caresses it, sleeps with it, celebrates it; it is one of his favourite toys and his most steadfast love. True, there is perhaps as much fear in his attitude as in that

4

of others, but at least death is not hidden away: he looks at it face to face, with impatience, disdain or irony.'

According to Paz, the Mexican is not afraid of death because he does not value life. Be that as it may, the dead are given their own fiesta; the brightly coloured skulls made of sugar, plaster and papier mâché, provide an ironic commentary on life and death. They grin broadly at both, and provide a reminder that, though life is brief, death and life are part of a continuous cycle. Writing on death, Montaigne mentions the ancient Egyptians, 'who, at the height of their feasting and mirth caused a dried skeleton of a man to be brought into the room to serve as a memento to their guests'. But a memento of what? Of the ever-present reality of death, of course, but with what result? Surely not to cast a pall over the feast, but rather to make its lamps burn the brighter, its grapes burst more sweetly on the tongue. So the universal message of the skull (Mexican, Egyptian, or carved in an English country churchyard) transcends the terror of 'Remember you must die'. It is, as well, an urgent exhortation: *Carpe Diem*, or 'Gather ye Rosebuds while ye may'.

Montaigne quotes Cicero: 'To philosophize is to learn to die'. Yet, perhaps understandably, most people shy away from any contemplation of death. When I mentioned that I was making a series of programmes about the effects of bereavement on certain individuals the response was normally disbelief that I should choose to embark on so gloomy a project. If I replied that the conversations I have had about death and love, far from being depressing, were uplifting, moving and sometimes even joyful, I saw (in many cases) the eyes slide away. Then I wondered how my interlocutor would respond if his neighbour's wife died, or if her colleague's friend was killed: would the road be crossed quickly to avoid a confrontation with grief? It seems to me that although such evasiveness may be understandable, it diminishes humanity and expresses the essentially frivolous modern requirement to be collectively 'happy' at all costs. The fear of death may in fact represent a terror of seriousness. I believe that the turning-away from death, and grief, is a denial of the essence of experience. As

Jung comments in *The Soul and Death*, 'The negation of life's fulfilment is synonymous with the refusal to accept its ending. Both mean not wanting to live; not wanting to live is identical with not wanting to die. Waxing and waning make one curve'.

To those locked into an extremity of grief, such philosophical pronouncements could seem glib. Yet I found again and again that those bereaved would have welcomed real understanding from the rest of the world – an understanding which can only be reached through personal experience or by being courageous enough to reach out towards the experiences of others. In her study, *Death and the Family*, Lily Pincus emphasizes the difficulty of believing in death: 'one of the major tasks of mourning, accepting the reality of loss'. It is especially difficult when you have not *seen* – when, for instance, a friend dies in a plane crash, or when (as Christopher Booker describes here) a sister is killed on the other side of the world. You know it is true, as an objective fact, but the heart cannot take in what the mind is forced to acknowledge. There is a vacuum: a still point of emptiness around which potentially corrosive emotions like guilt, resentment, or blind confusion, swirl. As Pincus says, 'bereavement brings about a crisis of loss, probably the most severe crisis in human existence.'

There is no easy formula for coping. But all current psychological expertise agrees that a start is made by allowing yourself to mourn, and the time to see that mourning through. 'Mourning is no longer a necessary period, imposed by society', writes Philippe Aries, 'it has become a *morbid state* which must be treated, shortened, erased by the "doctor of grief".' Friends will urge you to 'Pull yourself together', or 'Look to the future and get on with life', or use any of the other phrases of awkward evasion, uttered to protect the speaker. But what needs to be said is, 'This is real, this is true, and this will never ever go away – not completely.' Only then is the loss, and the love, fully honoured. When the bereaved one cries out, inwardly or outwardly, 'I would give anything just to see her (or him) again', what is speaking is the voice of love. Love cries out for immortality to be true, so that one day it will be able to see the loved one again. Or love declares it *knows* immortality to be true, in that, the first anguish of grief over, the beloved dead are felt to be there, each day, all around. Human life rests upon love. And love, if you like, is evidence – incontrovertible evidence, for Christian and agnostic alike – of immortality.

The 'good death' used to refer to the nature of a person's dying, the noble quality of which might even serve to expiate previous sins. The 'good death' might also be said to be the nature of a particular death as experienced by the bereaved. Allowed to mourn, allowing themselves to mourn and to understand, they can even achieve the seemingly miraculous – transmuting loss into gain. Death can offer those who are left a totally new perspective for living. Death can play the role of a stern yet benign teacher, but only if certain conditions are fulfilled. The bereaved person has to be able to express grief, to accept the loss, to understand the significance of survival and so, in effect, build a life from the death. Finally, through a fuller understanding of life he/she has to be able to face his/her own mortality.

Although each individual death is, of course, unique, it unites both the living and the dead with the universe. The universals of grief are timeless, and transcend class and culture. Reading the accounts in this book one can identify common strands which might be echoed again and again in countless such conversations: the consolations of ritual, the need to talk about the loss, the different stages as well as the subtle permanence of grief, and the sense of being removed by the experience on to a different plane. Each person acknowledges the implacable reality of death, but demonstrates also a strength of feeling, of wisdom, which transcends it.

In making the two series we attempted to cover a range of experience, so that each account would be at once personal and also strike a chord with others. So the quiet regret expressed by Chris Patten and Daniel Topolski at the death of (respectively) mother and father will be familiar to many, as will the gentle pride expressed by Clare Short, whose father's death intensified for her a powerful belief in humanistic immortality – the perpetual nature of human goodness. In contrast with these undramatic accounts are three parents talking about the death of a child, and yet, through searing grief, it is significant that neither Barrie Rutter, Val Hazel nor Anna Haycraft protest that death came too soon. Clearly they reject the idea that life is a parking meter, that there is an allotted time. Lord Hailsham and Pamela Gillilan describe the acute loneliness following the death of a life-partner, although their conclusions are very different. Anne Chisholm's sister died of cancer, and Bernard Levin remembers the slow self-destruction of a friend who was an alcoholic. In addition it seemed to me important to address the modern phenomenon of AIDS, and so Tony Whitehead discusses the death of his lover George. Since violent death is something most people dread, especially in a news dominated age, we included Christopher Booker's story of the murder of his sister. The conversations were sometimes extremely painful, for both participants; I should add that our intention in making the programmes was not voyeuristic and so any audible evidence of grief was pruned.

When you are bereaved you cry, again and again, 'Why me?', until the quiet moment when you suddenly turn the question on its head: 'Why *not* me?' Or, 'That which is only living can only die'. To reflect thus is not to diminish the pain of loss, or to take mortality less than seriously. It is to accept that death lives beneath the surface of the skin, and each beat of the heart announces its presence. Bereavement may leave you bleak and bitter for a while, and demented, angry, disappointed, guilty. It also places you permanently on the interface between suffering and acceptance, bestowing the knowledge that death is simultaneously an individual outrage and something which is, after all, quite ordinary.

And that is a thought which is not only uniting, but profoundly consoling too. His mother, her son, my child, your father . . . all mourned; this husband, that wife, this friend, that son . . . all mourning, yet stumbling, perhaps, towards an understanding of the mystery which is at the core of all philosophical and religious systems of thought. And it is a terrible mistake for us to shy away from their grief and their knowledge, because it can enlarge even those who have had no experience of death. This reaching-out, and being part of the whole should be celebrated with reverence, not denied.

# Author's Note

The first series of *A Perspective For Living* was broadcast in Spring 1991, and repeated later the same year. We recorded about fifty minutes of conversation, and edited it to a twenty-eight-minute programme. The six interviews – with Chris Patten, Anna Haycraft, Pamela Gillilan, Bernard Levin, Barrie Rutter and Anne Chisholm – are transcribed here as broadcast, with a minimum of 'tidying' to allow for the demands of reader, as distinct from listener. The second series was recorded early in 1992, and these six conversations – with Christopher Booker, Lord Hailsham, Clare Short, Tony Whitehead, Val Hazel and Daniel Topolski – were taken, with necessary cutting and tidying, from the unedited tapes. They are, therefore, longer than the interviews actually broadcast at the end of 1992 and in places somewhat different. Thanks are due to Tim Sutor, for suggesting the idea, and to each series producer, Beaty Rubens and Penny Lawrence, for being so sympathetic to work with, providing suggestions with tact and intelligence. I should add that it is not always easy to talk about one's feelings in a radio studio, as these twelve people did. They willingly agreed to do so, and gave their permission for these transcripts to be published, because they felt that their experiences might be useful to others. The letters from listeners were proof that they were right, and I am deeply grateful to them all.

The extract from *The Birds of the Air* by Alice Thomas Ellis is reprinted by permission of Gerald Duckworth Ltd. The poems by Pamela Gillilan are reprinted by permission of Bloodaxe Books Ltd. from *That Winter*, Bloodaxe, 1986.

# 1

# CHRISTOPHER BOOKER

*The writer Christopher Booker, columnist with the* Sunday
Telegraph, *remembers his sister Serena, who was murdered
on a trip to Thailand.*

I grew up originally thinking that the sort of natural size of a
human family was four. I had father, mother and myself and a
sister eighteen months younger than me. It was something of a
shock to us when I was seventeen and my mother (at the age of
42) had a third child, a daughter. She was born in 1954 in the
middle of a great thunderstorm in a girls' school in Dorset about
five yards from a dormitory full of small girls and that was my
younger sister Serena – or Cly as she was called, Clytemnestra.

It was a rather extraordinary, rather ominous thing that her
elder sister, Joanna (who was very interested in Greek tragedy),
took to calling her Clytemnestra shortly after she'd been born,
and in the way that nicknames do in families this stuck. It was
shortened to Cly and she remained Cly to her friends and to her
family the rest of her life.

*So she was much younger than you. Did you feel protective towards her?*

Oh yes. It was very odd having a sister quite so much younger,
but as she grew up she was a very strong-willed person; actually,
she was a dominant person and from the earliest of ages she was
trying to boss everyone around and you were very much aware of
her presence. I think it was not 'til I was out at a restaurant with

her when she was in her teens and I suddenly heard someone banging on in a rather intelligent fashion about aid to the Third World or something and I thought, 'Good heavens that's my little sister Cly,' and it was the moment when I suddenly realized that she wasn't just a little girl, a little child anymore, she was actually becoming an adult. In her adult years I became very close to her; we had a lot of interests in common.

After reading history at university she went off to work in Vienna, and she then came back in 1979 to do research. She was hired by Alistair Horne to assist him with the research on his Life of Harold Macmillan.

*Were your parents proud of her?*

Immensely proud of her, yes, and this became reinforced when in 1976 our other sister, Joanna, who was only eighteen months younger than me, died in tragic, difficult circumstances. She was a mother of three small children and it was obviously a terrible blow to others, but for my parents losing a daughter like that was a ghastly blow. After that, Serena, who was very devoted to her parents, spent a lot of time trying to sort of – not make up to them for what they'd lost – but she used to take them on holidays, for instance. She'd make sure that they got a decent long holiday in Brittany or Greece or somewhere each year and she would accompany them and take them round and make sure that they got booked into hotels and saw all the right things. So not only were my parents proud of Cly but she became very much a sort of support, more than a lot of daughters would be to parents. She was in her twenties by this time, mid-twenties.

*Tell me what happened in 1982.*

She'd been working extremely hard, firstly on Alistair Horne's book on Macmillan, then for Robert Rhodes James who had to write the official Life of Anthony Eden. She did an amazing amount of work in 1982 and eventually felt she must get away for a holiday; she had a very strong compulsion to travel. She liked travelling alone; she'd done a lot around Europe and North Africa and thought that for the first time in her life she'd go to the East. She particularly wanted to go to Burma which was a difficult country to get into. I don't know whether this is still true, but you could only get into Burma through Thailand, so she realized that she would have to go to Thailand first, and – well to cut a long story short she set off in September 1982.

She flew to Bangkok and she knew that she wanted to see quite a lot of Thailand on her way up to the Burmese frontier, so instead of going up by 'plane she decided she would travel up through the middle of Thailand by bus. She arrived at a little market town about half-way up and she was looking for someone who could take her to a temple. She'd done a lot of homework before she went on what sites she wanted to see and she particularly wanted to see ancient Buddhist temples and there was only one taxi driver in the town who spoke English and so he volunteered to take her to this place which was a few miles outside the town. And no one knows exactly how it happened or what happened but an hour or two later the taxi driver returned saying that an English tourist had been murdered in a particularly brutal fashion, and when the police questioned him they became increasingly suspicious that he in fact had done it himself. His story didn't hold together and she was found there, and she had indeed been killed.

It was two or three days before the word got to Bangkok and finally the British police were told and the word came through to my parents. I got to know about it because I was leaving my study in Somerset to go and post some letters and the telephone rang and it was in such a way that normally I would have probably let it ring 'cos I was already half-way out of the house, but some voice inside me said, 'This telephone call is going to change your life, answer it,' and I came to the telephone and it was my mother sounding very broken saying that a policeman wanted to talk to me, and he said, 'I've just had to come and tell your parents that your sister has been found murdered in Thailand.' The funny thing was that because we'd lost our other sister a few years before, my first reaction was to think, 'Hang on, they've got the wrong girl'. But they hadn't.

*What was the immediate effect on you after that? I presume you had to go to your parents. . . ?*

The immediate thing which took over was – because I'd been through the death of my other sister those years earlier I'd had some experience of how there are all sorts of practical, immediate things one must do.

As soon as I'd gone to see my parents and found out what little we knew, I discovered that one of the first really awful practical details which had to be dealt with was that they required identification of my sister. Her body was in this little town in the middle of Thailand but nothing could be further done until it had been absolutely proved to legal satisfaction that it was her. So an extraordinary, rather gruesome drama began to unfold. My first thought was I should fly out, and I took advice from one or two people as my sister had done. Before she went she had been advised by two people who knew Thailand very well that it was a very dangerous country, particularly dangerous for a female Western tourist and she was not to go alone through the country, and of course she had not taken that advice. Now one of those people I immediately got on to and I asked, 'Look should I fly out? My parents are in a terrible state, I ought to be here to look after them, but on the other hand we've got to get my sister identified.' He said, 'I know Thailand, it's a very hot country, and without going into too many of the details there are all sorts of reasons why, if you can find another way to get her identified, I think you should stay here and stay with your parents and not get lost out there for several days.'

So we still had to do the identification and it looked as if we were going to have to do it through photographs which had been taken of her body, and the Foreign Office was involved, and more than a week went by and these photographs never came. In the end Terry Waite intervened, and a miraculous figure emerged from this sea of confusion who was our Deputy Consul in Bangkok who said, 'Look, dental records will be enough.' I found my sister's dentist in Sloane Street and that was enough: we didn't need the photographs, didn't need me to go out there. He then took over the business of getting her remains brought back to England and it was decided for two practical reasons that she should be cremated in Bangkok and he arranged that. She was cremated in a Buddhist temple.

*Is that what she would have wanted?*

Yes. That is one of the two reasons why it was done. One was simple convenience. It would have been actually very complicated, as many people have found, to bring a full coffin from far away across the world. The other extraordinary thing my sister had done a month before she went to Thailand was this: she had written out a very long letter which in effect was like a will. As I've said she was a very bossy, dominant person, always ordering us all around, and one of the amazing things when she died was we found this letter which was marked to be opened in case something happened when she was abroad. It's not often that a twenty-seven year old going on holiday writes in effect a last will and testament. What it did was give complete instructions as to what was to happen to all her belongings. She also gave very detailed instructions as to what was to happen if anything did happen to her when she was abroad, including that she wanted her body to be cremated without a coffin, which of course would be illegal in this country. But in fact, as it happened, she was burned in that form on a funeral pyre in the courtyard of the temple in Bangkok. So she had her instructions followed in that respect without anyone having really to intervene; it couldn't have been any other way. She also laid down a rather complicated series of things she wanted done with her ashes, and it took us more than a year to actually carry out all those instructions.

*What did she want?*

She wanted some of her ashes to be buried in the churchyard of the little village in Dorset where we all grew up and she wanted some to be scattered around the hills and the valleys which she had loved riding over during her teens and which we'd all loved. It's a very, very beautiful part of the Stour Valley. The other thing was that her time in Austria in Vienna had meant a great deal to her heart and particularly because of one friendship she had out there and she wanted the remains of her ashes, if such were left, to be scattered in various places in the Vienna Woods and around the Danube bend – which of course is one of the most beautiful places in the world. So my mother and I had this melancholy task, but in the end it turned out to be a very moving and memorable experience to go out to Vienna and to carry out my sister's orders and requests in a beautiful October with the Vienna Woods looking absolutely their gorgeous Autumn best. And we did it with some of her friends and the whole thing became a very solemn sort of act of remembrance of her, and I thought at the end, 'Isn't that clever of her to suggest that we should do that?'

There was one particular place in the Vienna Woods – there's the hill which falls away down to the city of Vienna and you're surrounded with the trees and the road curves round at the top of this hill past a little wayside crucifix – and I thought this is a perfect place because of the wonderful view of Vienna down below, to scatter some of her ashes. So I walked over to the edge, just underneath the crucifix, and scattered them in some bracken and at the moment I did so the sun was golden and as I scattered the ashes, a deer leapt out of the bracken about literally five or six feet from where I was standing and it bounded away down the hill in a series of great graceful leaps. It was like a great sort of burst of life coming out of that very solemn moment. It was wonderful.

*Did you find that consoling?*

I did. I told my friend Laurence Van der Post about it; it's the kind of thing which he would see significance in, quite rightly. I remember he consoled me greatly because he said also, 'It's very important that she died in a temple. Remember she died on holy ground.' I've been consoled by that thought. I mean, obviously it's a violation of holy ground, but it did help in reconstructing the absolutely awful circumstances in which she died to get that part of the picture firmly in focus – that it was a holy place.

*I want to talk a little bit more about consolation but before we reach that I want to ask you if in the months after her death you felt any desire for revenge – in all the anger that there must have been at the way she died?*

I'll tell you a very curious thing. I've been actually profoundly grateful that the one thing I didn't feel, and I don't think my parents felt, was any desire for revenge. I know how natural and powerful it can be. I didn't feel that, but on the other hand, something very strange happened. There was this man who was suspected by the police of having killed my sister and they arrested him and charged him with the murder. They then let him out on bail and his trial was eventually fixed for about a year after the murder had taken place, and that is an odd thing enough in itself. But the oddest thing of all was that two weeks before his trial was due to begin, when he was due to come back to this town to be tried for murder, his body was found in another part of Thailand with seventeen bullets in it, and nobody could explain it. It was thought that he'd actually got involved in drugs or something and, of course, parts of Thailand are extremely violent. So although I didn't feel any desire for revenge at the time, I have to say that I do feel an obscure satisfaction that the account was settled, and I'm just grateful that I didn't feel that I had to be part of that settling. It happened because Providence ordained it thus. But I can absolutely understand why people do feel . . . because if one human being kills another there's no question, if you write that in a story, it's very hard to bring the story to a satisfactory resolution until the murderer is called to account in some way. You can't have the murderer wandering off happily at the end of the story; you feel that some cosmic law has been violated.

*There's a need for punishment?*

There is a need for punishment, in storytelling certainly: a death leads to a death unless there is eventually some great act of expiation or remorse.

*Was there a great difference in yourself in the way that you responded to your younger sister's death as contrasted with the tragic death of your older sister some years before?*

I think having lived through one awful time when, on reflection afterwards, I'd thought that I hadn't really done some of the things I should have done and I hadn't said some of the things I should have said – all sorts of things, ways, in which I'd failed – I did feel almost as soon as I knew about Serena, Cly's, death, 'I've really got to do my stuff this time. I've got to do it on behalf of other people.' I obviously knew that my parents would need very special care and there were a lot of practical things to be done with proper efficiency, but in addition to that there is one of the most important things that comes out of a death.

Can I just say I had a particular problem that week? I was in a very unusual position because I had to write a column in the *Daily Telegraph*. I did it every month and it just happened that that was the week when I had to write it; it allowed one to be very personal about things that one had experienced. So I knew the moment my sister died I could either write about my sister's death or I would have to not do the column, because obviously it just blotted everything else out. So I decided I would write about it and I wrote an article called 'Incident in Thailand' and it was really a picture of her life as a wonderfully lively, bubbling person who was loved by many, and it was only towards the end in the last two or three paragraphs that I described how the news had come through of what had happened to her in Thailand. The response to that from the readers of the *Telegraph* was absolutely astonishing: over the next few weeks we had something like six hundred letters and that was an infinite consolation. What struck me about them was how personally people had reacted, I mean, many of the people who wrote to me were people who'd been through a tragedy in their own lives. Those were the letters which really stood out because as soon as you've been through something like that you can share something with other people who are also in that position, which is obviously hard if you haven't been in that land. I was so struck by how individual they were. We're often told that letter writing as an art is dead these days, but if you look through those letters one after another, quite different from each other, each one describing their own experiences using words of consolation, not in a sort of bland, empty formula of condolence but actual living feelings coming across . . . And they were a wonderful, wonderful consolation, those letters; so much so that I've written two or three times since about how important it is to write when someone has died, not necessarily tragically. I've had this experience subsequently with the deaths of both of my parents, both of whom (because they had been involved in education and had a very wide circle of former pupils and friends) attracted a lot of very loving and admiring and grateful letters. Hugely important that was to me, and I know from talking to other people just how important that is when there has been a death.

*Although each death is unique, as we know it to be, do you think there's a universal common factor which enables people's spirits to touch each other in that way?*

Yes. A phrase which I use because it has come back to me again and again on all these occasions is the 'community of grief'. It does bring people together.

*It occurs to me that you have been questionably privileged to enter the*

*community of grief more than once. I mean, you've had the death of two*
*sisters and then both parents – is there a sense in which you've ever felt*
*that it wasn't fair, that you've had too much of a burden?*

I felt that very much on behalf of my parents because to lose two
of three children is obviously a particular blow, but they're by no
means alone in that. I remember there was one family I read of, of
seven children and the two parents, and within ten years there
were only two left; and Geoffrey Grigson the writer had six
brothers who died in the First World War (he was the seventh).
So it's quite a common experience, but you do get changed
enormously by the experience of the deaths of people close to you.
You have to respond to them in certain ways, and you grow
through living through someone else's death, someone close to
you. I know that I've felt that because there's been a sequence of
deaths in my own life and as it's gone on . . . this is terribly hard
to put; I'm sorry I'm collapsing again.

*Do you think it's important – is this something you've learnt from your*
*own experience – that one should prepare oneself for one's own death?*
*I'm actually thinking back to your younger sister's death. She wrote*
*that letter as if she had a premonition.*

I answer that in two ways which are oblique to each other. Firstly
it was one of the extraordinary things about Cly's death that she
had written this very remarkable set of instructions a month
earlier as to what should happen if for any reason she died while
she was abroad. When something like that happens it seems such
a sort of inexplicable bolt from the blue, such a terrible thing that
someone close to you has been murdered, particularly when it's
on holiday far away and there's sort of no immediate reason why
it should have happened. So you look for any reasons. 'Is there any
explanation for this?' you say to yourself. In my sister's case it
appeared that somehow it had been foreshadowed. There'd been
premonitions. She herself had written this extraordinary letter.
Other people had had terrific feelings of foreboding about her

going. I could go into other reasons, but there were all sorts of ways in which she spent the last three days of her time in England going round to see all her friends in a way that you wouldn't normally do if you were going off on just an ordinary two-week holiday in France. She went to say goodbye to everybody who'd meant something to her and she ended up on the last afternoon in a garden in Wiltshire on a sunny September afternoon meeting someone whom she had long wanted to meet: the glass engraver Laurence Whistler. They sat under an ash tree for five hours in the sunshine and they had an absolutely magical conversation which meant a great deal to both of them, and then she went off the following day and the following Thursday she was murdered.

One of the things that grew out of that was a number of her friends felt very strongly a desire to mark her death with a memorial of some kind that would enable us to remember her; and very early the idea came into the minds of at least two people that it might be an idea to get a window engraved by Laurence Whistler. When the idea was put to him he said the moment that he'd heard of her death he'd already begun to design not one window but two, and they were to commemorate both my sisters, and he said it was because the conversation with her had meant so much to him and he was absolutely stunned when he heard she'd died. So that became a very important thing because I'd already been an admirer of Laurence Whistler's exquisite jewel-like engravings and my sister had known a lot of them. That project, which took about three years, became an enormous source of consolation because I could see what Laurence was trying to do: two works of art which he was engraving on glass, which were of really extraordinary beauty and enormous profundity. We discussed some of the details but obviously it was fundamentally his own inner vision. The two pictures showed a Dorset landscape – the country we'd grown up in – and both of them had a rose over the top of them. Streaming light and the idea of a rose being the source of light . . .

They were originally going to be in one church and then there were all sorts of problems and eventually the Dean of Salisbury asked whether we'd like to put them in Salisbury Cathedral, which of course is an extraordinary honour. So for three years we had this whole saga of seeing this work of art created and then finally put in that marvellous place. That in itself became something that transmuted the whole experience of grief. It helped it, there's no question. Out of the darkness we were able to spin something of beauty, of light, which actually helped to elevate us all greatly.

*Symbolism seems to be very important to you. You talked about the deer in Austria and now the glass panels. Does that help you to make sense of death itself?*

I find from my own experience that I do look for symbols because they concentrate the immediate pain and meaninglessness and suffering, and start to give it some kind of meaning and purpose and a structure; and they also start to restore a sense of life out of these horrible dark experiences. I mean, what is symbolism? It is simply the mediating thing. I mentioned the deer bounding away and that gave me a tremendous sense of life; it was an outward event, and I haven't got any theory as to how and why it happened. I found it was just a wonderful, miraculous, life-giving thing to see that deer bounding away down the hill. Similarly, this process of seeing Laurence Whistler's wonderful meditations in glass was similar, at a deeper level and over a longer period of time. They were inspired by the deaths of my sisters but like any great work of art became something much more universal. The phrase which continually comes to my mind is From Darkness into Light. Laurence himself used the phrase. He said the light needs the darkness to become articulate. And that for me is the most important thing about living through tragedies so close to one: that actually through that darkness you do come to see. They give you the chance to find the light. It's very hard, of course, because you're plunged into darkness, but the light does need the darkness to become articulate.

I have to say, I started from a position of having a religious view of the world so in no way was it a conversion. But all these experiences have immeasurably deepened my appreciation of this great polarity between death and life, and darkness and light, and how the true light is something eternal and shines forever out of these specific, awful, imprisoning experiences which leave one so confused. In the end the most important thing was to find meaning in them. Why did they happen? And the death of my sister which was on the face of it a totally inexplicable meaningless event eventually came to be surrounded with so many premonitions and foreshadowings that I came to see that it had to be. She had to go to Thailand. She knew she was going to die. It did not seem any longer to be a meaningless event. It seemed to be something which, however ghastly, however unspeakable, however hard to take for the rest of us, was something which was long prefigured in her life.

*Is there any sense in which, then, you came to see her death as almost a necessary sacrifice in order to achieve growth?*

I've meditated on that one. I know that I have gained greatly from the experience of these deaths but I wouldn't dream of putting it quite like that. All I'm saying is that there is no such thing as an untimely death. I think when we start to see what that means in our own lives we've attained a little bit of wisdom. You want to be able to see that it wasn't just an inexplicable event, that it was part of some great pattern. I don't think that the deaths of these people close to me were in any way necessary, I just think they were things which were part of some wider pattern. So I accept that and I also know that I have grown out of them.

*I wasn't thinking just of you; I was thinking of the people who loved your sister as well and the people who will see the Whistler windows – it goes broader, doesn't it? Even all the people who wrote to you who felt that your experience had touched their own.*

Ah well, that's right. Now you're talking about a huge number of people involved on the edge of, or towards the centre of deaths and bereavements and tragedies. Ultimately one either doesn't respond and walks away inwardly and it just leaves you untouched, or if you do get involved in active bereavement and mourning and grief it is something that we grow through – all of us. Even in the act of writing a letter to someone who's been bereaved (if it becomes a living letter and not a dead set of words), you are having an experience which is important to the person who's receiving the letter. If you're a writer you're there to produce words. It is a wonderful thing to have the chance to be able to reflect on the merits of someone that one has known and loved and to describe their life and to see meaning in it and see significance in both their life and perhaps even in their death.

*A lot of people who have experienced bereavement might find themselves thinking that you're a very fortunate person because you're able to express it in words, and because you had a Christian faith already, and because you were able to extract meaning from the appalling tragedy, whilst they might feel themselves lost in the Valley of the Shadow. On behalf of those who actually feel totally negative when they're bereaved – feel angry and guilty – did you ever feel that it was only bleak and black, at some stage?*

Of course, it was totally bleak and black. I'm talking now reflectively after years, about what eventually came out of those experiences, but if I go back into those experiences the whole point is that at the time they're happening and perhaps for weeks and months, sometimes for years afterwards, one is in a total utter chaos of puzzlement and despair and horror and sadness and grief. I hope I haven't given the impression that I immediately sprang to: 'The meaning of this is such and such. Yes, this was an intended event.' I don't mean any of that. I mean these are the conclusions one eventually painfully wins through to.

*Have the deaths that you've experienced helped you to prepare for your own?*

28

Not particularly, no. The only thing that I ever dwell on in preparing for my own death is a dream I had many years ago where I was blown up by an H-Bomb with four other people, four Indians, and at the moment when this awful thing took place, I felt myself being carried up into a great cloud of light; and it was light and it was love and it was total release from this world, and it was a moment of inexpressible joy and bliss. Now this is a personal dream and that for me is the only consolation. I have no vision of the other side or what happens there, but I do have some kind of a vision of a release from this earthly life which is not just a black hole of nothingness but something inexplicable – to be absorbed into life itself, 'the love that moves the sun and the other stars'.

*Do you feel that you'll see the people you love there? Does it take that shape?*

I don't see it in personal terms. I see it as being reabsorbed into the energy of the universe in some quite mysterious and extraordinary way, but on the other hand I know that it is important to many people to see the after-life in personal terms. I'm totally ignorant about it. I listen with great interest to people who talk about any kind of indication that people can come back. Who knows? Nobody does on this earth and I wouldn't ever pronounce in any kind of arbitrary fashion on these things. One can only talk about what has meaning to oneself.

*It interests me that Serena had gone to see a Buddhist temple and, as you described, had been cremated in the Buddhist way, as if she was following that path. Did she believe in recurrence?*

Not at all. I don't know what her religious views were really. She was a sort of practising member of the Church of England. She wasn't terrifically given to metaphysical speculations. I will tell you one thing though, at the moment when I knew that she was being cremated in Bangkok I went up to my local village church in Somerset because I just wanted to be there to meditate at the moment when I knew the thing was taking place. I had asked the Consul in Bangkok to take a huge bunch of red roses and put them on to be burnt at the same time. And as I left the house to go up the road to the church I pulled out a book almost at random; I didn't take a Bible or the poems of John Donne. When I looked at the book there must have been something more than random because I had pulled out the poems of T.S. Eliot. And at the moment when my sister's body was being burned, at eleven o'clock, I found myself looking at some lines from the last of the Four Quartets, 'Little Gidding', including the great consolation of Mother Julian: 'all shall be well and all manner of thing shall be well'. Several bits of that struck me as being particularly relevant and, of course, it ends with 'the fire and the rose are one'. And that hit me because it was at that moment that the roses that I'd asked for presumably were with Serena's body being consumed by the fire.

When I got in touch with Laurence Whistler about the possibility of doing the panels, I said that I'd read at her funeral (when her remains came back to England) these lines from 'Little Gidding'. He said, 'Well, I've already started to put some lines from 'Little Gidding' in my design.'

*Do those coincidences ever frighten you?*

No, they don't frighten me at all. I think that the more one is in touch with one's centre, the more deeply one is aware of this web of meaning and coincidence and symbolism and omen. I think it's there all the time. I know that there are many periods in my life when I become preoccupied with daily things and live a selfish, superficial life and get blind to that side of things. But deaths obviously shake one out of one's normal humdrum frame of existence. It is extraordinary how things do hit one simultaneously, and I marvel at it because it's part of the reassurance that there is a purpose and a meaning to everything and everything is really all part of the same great story.

*With the idea of meaning very much in mind, do you ever feel that you have to live for these spirits who are your family?*

Yes I'm certainly aware of their presence, as it were, without being in any way able to define what that means. When someone close to you has died you think of them looking over your shoulder quite often, and wonder, 'What would they make of this?'

*Do you think that perhaps we have all gone too far down the road of agreeing with John Donne that 'Any man's death diminishes me' and that perhaps we ought to see it in a more positive way: that any man's death can enlarge me?*

Very much so. I think we *are* enlarged by people's deaths. I mean obviously we're diminished in the sense that they are torn away from us, we've lost them, lost their earthly presence, and we have to start looking at them in a wholly new way. But as well as diminishing, death certainly can enhance, enlarge, our lives, so long as we live through properly and openly and fully, and don't try and run away from it, or shut it out, but accept that there it is. It is absolutely in the centre of all lives, both the deaths of others and our own death eventually. I think we experience life more richly and deeply through a proper approach to the deaths of others, and eventually, of course, our own.

# 2

# ANNE CHISHOLM

*The biographer and journalist Anne Chisholm talks about
her sister Clare, who died of cancer.*

I was the oldest in the family. There was me and then my sister
Clare, five years younger, and a brother four years younger
again.

*Did you get on with your sister?*

Yes I did. Five years is quite a big gap, especially when you're
growing up, and we were very different: different physically,
different approach to life, different temperament. And in the
family there was one of those rather unhelpful situations that
well-meaning parents can sometimes bring about, in which I was
the clever one and she was the pretty one. It could have made
trouble but actually on the whole didn't, because the gap was
wide enough and we made our own lives.

*Were you ever jealous of her?*

I do remember being jealous of her being so stunningly pretty
when she was about thirteen and I was about eighteen and just
beginning to feel I'd like to be stunningly beautiful; and I could
see then that she was going to grow into the kind of beauty that
made people gasp when she came into the room. She was very,

very beautiful. But she was also quite jealous that I was supposed to be cleverer and won scholarships and things.

*Did you ever say that to each other?*

Oh no, no, no, we didn't.

*So you didn't have a very close relationship in terms of frankness?*

I was always a much more talkative person about emotional things than Clare was. Clare was quite self-contained, quite proud, in a way quite shy. I mean, I tend to talk about myself to anyone at the drop of a hat but she wasn't like that. One of the sad things about what happened was that I felt that we were getting closer in that way around the time she died.

*How old was she then?*

She was twenty-nine.

*And what was she doing with her life? What was her job?*

Well, she'd been to art school, met a man by whom she had a child, dropped out of art school and became a model. This was in the early Sixties and it was all a very Sixties event and she and this man were this wonderful-looking young couple and they didn't worry about degrees or qualifications or careers and they wore a lot of beads and were rather sort of feckless and charming. And she was a very successful model, first in America and then in London with top model agencies, made a very great deal of money and travelled and so on. She found it amusing for a while, then I think was getting bored, and had a child which made it harder to travel and live that kind of irresponsible life. And again, you know, part of the sadness of what happened to her was that I think she was beginning to decide that she would like to do something else and she had started talking about perhaps doing a course or moving out of modelling, when she got ill.

*Before we talk about her illness can I pick out two particular words you used there: 'feckless' and 'irresponsible'. At the time did you disapprove of her?*

I don't think I disapproved of her. I recognized she was very different from me and I worried about her. I think I had rather the older sister sort of protectiveness which she didn't much care for, but we never fought about it. I mean I never tried to change her life, I couldn't have even if I had wanted to, but possibly there was a little bit of tension there. It was never anything that was a problem.

*At that stage in your life were you married? Successful?*

I was not married, but settled with someone. I was a freelance journalist, writing a book. And she was living on her own because that relationship had broken up. So at that point I was very much the settled one and she was very much in a state of transition.

*And what happened then?*

She went to see the doctor one day and was told there was some minor, as she thought, gynaecological problem and she had to go into hospital and have it looked at. And in fact, I was abroad. I was researching a book and I was on a trip in France in a hotel in Toulouse where I was going to be joined by a girlfriend – we were going to have a few days off in the Dordogne looking around the house of the subject of my book – and I got a 'phone call to say that Clare had been to hospital and it had been discovered that she hadn't got a minor problem, she'd got a major problem, and they were going to keep her in and do an operation and I should come home. It was one of those really extraordinary moments that you never, ever forget. I was in a cheap hotel in Toulouse, I think it was probably a brothel because there was a great deal of banging and squeaking of springs and shouting all around me and I was taking this 'phone call and listening to these weird and rather squalid noises, and I remember thinking, 'This is one of the worst moments of my life and what a very odd place to be.'

*And then did you go home?*

Yes, I went straight home. Then there was a fairly prolonged period of her having an operation and being told she had cancer and she had to have a complete hysterectomy followed by radiation treatment and they said with any luck they'd caught it, but they hadn't. This all happened in about April of that year and during the summer it was thought she might have a chance but in fact they discovered that the cancer was in her lymphatic system and I think we knew then that her chances weren't very good. But she did seem to get better and we went and spent much of the summer in a cottage in Norfolk that a friend lent, with her child who was four, and that was a good moment. It was the right thing to have done. I was glad I spent most of that summer with her, and then by the autumn she was getting worse and she was back in hospital and she died just before Christmas. So it all took barely eight, nine months.

*That summer, did she know she was going to die?*

No, I think that summer we were all hoping, and to some extent pretending, that she would get better. She didn't want to talk about it. I mean, she and I were alone in this house with her child and a cat and friends coming and going and every now and again, because my instinct is to talk about things and I thought maybe she'd want to, I would try, but she was always very much not one to talk about it, so one has to respect that really. Of course I've wondered since whether I shouldn't have tried harder, not perhaps during the summer, but later when she was in hospital and actually dying.

*How did her son approach his mother's illness at that stage?*

Well I think a child of four doesn't notice, as far as we can tell. He was unaware that she was in and out of hospital and not well. He was a very happy, vigorous, easy child and seemed to be alright.

*Who looked after him when she was in hospital?*

I did. Because her life was rather confused as I've said and I was more settled, she used quite often to leave him with me for quite long periods from when he was a baby, I mean a month or two old, so I was much more used to looking after him than most aunts would be with a nephew, and it was curious because I remember thinking, 'Don't get too fond of this child, he's not your child.'

*During the period when she was well?*

Yes, when she was well.

*Because you were afraid of that feeling?*

I think because I was trying quite hard to have a child of my own and failing at that time. I had a series of miscarriages and I knew that I had always loved Jess anyway, but I loved him particularly because he was this charming child who I looked after quite a lot and I was beginning to worry that I wouldn't have my own child. But that didn't produce any tension between us, on the contrary it was a bond: my love for him and her need of someone to help look after him was a very strong, good thing.

*And did that grow stronger during that last summer?*

I think what was always unspoken between us was the feeling that if she didn't get better I would look after him and that possibly helped. I hope it did, but equally it was very delicate ground because it was impossible, we felt, I felt, to be explicit about it, to say to her, 'Don't worry, if you don't get better I'll look after him.' I mean, it was implicit not explicit.

*Because you had to maintain the illusion that she might get better?*

Yes, I think so. And later, when she was evidently dying and had said by one or two hints to me that she knew that I knew that she wasn't going to get better, I tried to convey to her that I wanted to do what she wanted by asking did she think it would be a good thing if he went to see his father? He was by this time living in America. And she said, 'No he's too young, perhaps later when he's older.' I think we both knew that I was actually saying, 'Look, do you want me to look after him or do you want his father to look after him?' So there was a strange sort of subtext to her dying which was the life of this child and the two things are very interconnected for me. Her life ebbing and my taking on the responsibility for his life.

*After she died, who told her son that she was dead?*

I did. He was staying with my parents in Ireland and I was in London going to see my sister every day and about ten days after she died they came back to London with him for her funeral. My mother hadn't been able to face telling him, which I didn't blame her for, but I knew that I had to tell him the minute he appeared.

That's another very clear picture in my mind of this beaming face coming up the stairs in our flat and having to take him and sit him down and say what I had to say. But he was marvellous, he was an incredibly resilient child; he looked a bit taken aback and asked one or two questions but never cried, never pursued it, just accepted it.

*What did he ask?*

The first thing he said was, 'Does everybody know?' And I said, 'Like who?' So he ran through: did his grandparents know, did a friend of his at nursery school? He seemed to need to know what the circle had gathered about it all. Curious question really. And the thing to do seemed to be to get on with cooking the fish fingers or whatever it was.

*So what was the immediate effect of Clare's death on your life?*

Well the immediate and most dramatic effect was that I inherited, as it were, her child. His father in America never particularly took any responsibility for what would happen. He left it to us. It just seemed natural, so that's what I did and of course that was an enormous emotional prop. I remember worrying at the time and thinking, 'There's this pyramid of emotion focused on this child and he must be protected from it as best I can. He mustn't be made to carry the burden for everybody, for my parents and me and everybody.' But children are so wonderfully strong in some ways, they just get on with it and he helped us all, but I have sometimes worried that this very small child was actually carrying too much.

*Because he represented her?*

I suppose so, or because we all needed him and caring for him got us through it all. I mean, I was busy with him. I was able therefore perhaps not to be as frozen in my tracks as I think otherwise I might have been, because it was particularly awful to see someone so young and beautiful destroyed before your eyes. In slow motion you saw this person just vanish and it was obviously very shocking.

*Was there any stage at which that made you feel a kind of rage or bitterness?*

I don't think I felt bitterness. I felt a sort of horror. I felt a sort of surprise I think, because I'd never actually in any way come close to death before, it had never been part of my life, and suddenly it was there day by day, week by week, month by month, the centre of my life and I saw it all very much in close up. She died in Westminster Hospital just before Christmas and it was particularly bleak and odd. There were a lot of limp decorations and half-empty wards and people going off for the holiday and they sort of tidied her into a side ward. They did their best, they were pretty good really, but it was all rather dreadful.

*After her death you were left with this child who you say you had inherited. That must have delighted you in a way? I use that word hesitantly because of the awful circumstances, but he obviously brought you joy.*

Oh he did very much, particularly since it turned out that I wasn't going to have a child of my own. I didn't give up trying but it didn't happen. But he was, and is, the most delightful, happy character. I'm not saying that bringing him up has been entirely problem free – it hasn't – but it did give me great joy and it did help me very much to come to terms with what had happened.

*There's an extraordinary symmetry about this situation, isn't there, that out of your sister's death you, as it were, were given this little person to look after? Did that ever make you feel guilty?*

Yes, it did a bit. I did feel it was wrong to enjoy having him quite so much at one stage, but then I reflected and thought, don't flagellate yourself over this, this is really ridiculous, you would never, ever have dreamed of this, it's the cards that have fallen this way. How marvellous that at least there is something positive, which is that there's a child who needs a mother and there's a woman who needs a child, and the fact that it's within the same family is wonderful. And I have sometimes wondered whether that explains my comparatively positive feelings about having seen death so closely, because I do feel in some ways that I was strengthened by it. Perhaps it's easy for me to feel that because something so evidently positive emerged for me, which was looking after Jess.

*Was there ever a sense in which, difficult though it might be to say, you felt that perhaps you were a better mother for him than your sister would have been?*

I never felt I was a better mother; I felt I had a better organized life and I felt that my comparative stability (eventually marrying the same man that I had been with and living happily with him and so on), the fact that the flat was the same, that life ticked over in a very humdrum way, was some balancing factor for him against the appalling emotional deprivation of losing his real mother. I've never kidded myself that I was actually able to be a real mother to him and we've never ever stopped mentioning her to him and he's never been under any illusions about exactly what happened. But you know what kids are like, one has to sort of explain things again and they forget, and then they don't want to talk about it, and then suddenly they do and then you have to go into it all again. But it's all been quite open.

*How did he explain you to his friends?*

This was very interesting because he never, ever called me Mummy, he always called me Anne which is how he'd known me from his birth and that was fine, but I noticed that he always referred to me as 'my mum' to his friends as he grew up and went to school. He never, ever hesitated, he just adopted whatever was the easiest thing that made him the same as everybody else, because none of them like to be that different. But I did once get a real shock when I went to collect him.

We'd been living abroad and we'd come back for the summer with him and I put him into a new school, which is why this happened I think. He was about eight, and he came rushing up, beaming, and said,

'Good, you're there. I want you tell Danny that you're not my real mother, because my real mother really is dead.' Beaming. And I reeled back slightly and said,

'Oh, do you really want me to? Alright.'

And up came this very abashed, anxious-looking child, being dragged up by Jess, and Jess was jumping up and down saying, 'I've bet him 10p that my real mother really is dead and you're not my real mother, so tell him, tell him, go on tell him!'

So I said, 'Well it is true, it's very sad but it's true,' and I suppose the child . . . I can't remember if he produced the 10p or not, but anyway Jess and I set off walking home and I really was quite taken aback.

And I made a speech about how of course it was absolutely the truth and it was right to tell the truth and it was fine that it had happened to him and there was nothing to be ashamed of, but it was an upsetting thing and it could frighten and upset other children who didn't know about it already. And it was a serious thing and he shouldn't make bets about it or tell his friends like that; it was alright to tell them but perhaps not quite like that. I don't think he listened to a word of it, I think he'd thought he'd had a triumph and got 10p, but I don't think he did it again. I reminded him about it the other day and he laughed like anything.

*Did he remember it?*

No he couldn't remember it.

*Did he remember his feelings in general at that time?*

No, I have asked him more than once, partly because I felt it was important to keep it an open subject and alive for him. I have from time to time brought it up and asked what he can remember and what he felt, but rather like my sister, he doesn't find it easy to talk about his feelings. I mean, what adolescent boy does really? So we never really get very far.

*Apart from the presence of Jess, was there anything that consoled you?*

Well I remember about three months after she died we went on holiday to Italy to a place that we loved and had been to many times before, and we went without Jess. He went to stay with his grandparents. And I remember the first or second night that we were in this house in Tuscany I had the most wonderful dream and I dreamt very vividly that Clare had turned up and had told me that I wasn't to feel so dreadful and anxious and miserable about it and that it was all alright and that she was alright. I suppose that is a sort of classic dream that people can have when they very much want to find some sort of resolution, and in my case want to feel that I was doing the right thing with Jess. She wasn't specific about Jess, she just said, 'Everything's alright and I'm alright and you're not to worry so much,' and that was a great comfort to me and I've often thought of it and I think it probably is rather elementary but it did help me a lot. And the other thing I think that helped me was the growing realization that I was stronger for having learnt what I learnt about facing up to death. That is something that has always stayed with me and I feel I did gain by going through that. I'm sorry now for friends of mine who still can't talk about it or think about it and almost approach death as if it's something that only happens to other people, and live their lives as if they're not going to be touched by it.

*What's the precise effect of thinking about it all the time?*

I suppose the obvious answer is that it makes you appreciate your life and your luck in still being alive and so on, but that's not quite what it's about I think. There's a beautiful medieval tomb in a church in the country, where we live some of the time, which has a superb figure of a woman in a beautiful gown with her jewels and crown and so on on the top and underneath, life size as she is, is one of those skeletons. It's not actually a complete skeleton but it's a corpse, a very shrunken corpse. I mean, a body that looks very much like someone who's dying of cancer; it reminds me of the way I saw my sister look the last time I saw her, and that object sums up in a way what I mean. I find it hard to put it in words but it's the co-existence of the beauty, the serenity, the perfect human form juxtaposed with the essential: what is underneath it all and what we are all going to be in due course. I find that comforting rather than horrifying.

*Of course such images were put there to instil horror and fear and you said that you contemplated her death with horror. But you've moved a long way from that?*

Yes I suppose I have. Of course, there are images and moments that I remember with pain and horror. I remember the worst thing was going through her bits and pieces that arrived in a bag from the hospital. There was this little piece of Basildon Bond blue writing paper on which she'd written over and over again, 'the pain will stop, the pain will stop, the pain will stop'. And the writing got more and more desperate, and this was a piece of evidence of someone absolutely *in extremis*. So it was the evidence of suffering that horrified me afterwards, rather than being reminded of the fact of death.

*And now?*

And now. Well it's fifteen years later and Jess has grown up and it hasn't all been perfect and there have been moments when I've actually felt quite cross. I've thought, 'Right Clare, where are you now that we're going through all this, how about this muddle, now what?' But I think about her constantly. I mean, there's never more than a day when I don't think about her, largely of course in connection with him. He's also grown up looking very like her which is a marvellous sort of reminder of her, and the sense of pointlessness of somebody dying young is reduced by this strapping, handsome, amiable, impossible boy. I've never felt bitter about it, and that's thanks to him really.

# 3

# PAMELA GILLILAN

*In 1979 Pamela Gillilan won the Cheltenham Festival
Poetry Prize. For twenty years she ran a successful interior
decoration business with her husband David. Her first book,*
That Winter, *was directly inspired by his death.*

It seems sad that David died relatively young because he was a very strong sort of man. At school he'd been captain of cricket and captain of football and all this sort of thing, but the thing that made me decide that he was the person that I might marry was that I admired his intelligence; and he was interested in things I was interested in. In fact we both were writing poetry when we met. I found some of his poems after he died but in the meantime we hadn't written anything at all. Twenty-five years without writing anything.

*And you'd been working together in a business.*

Yes, and we had had times when money was non-existent. We'd had to work really hard and I think a combination of hard work and bringing up three children in a quite creative sort of medium that we were in made it difficult for one to create anything else.

*Because you lived together and worked together and built up this
business, I suppose in a way your lives were more entwined than perhaps
the average married couple.*

Yes, at times twenty-four hours a day, really.

*And how long did that go on?*

Well, ever since we went to Cornwall. We went to Cornwall first in 1951 and then we got a little house and shop up on Bodmin Moor and we were just buying and selling things and doing them up and sort of learning our trade the hard way. We didn't know what trade we were learning but that's how it turned out. We taught ourselves to do upholstery by taking things to pieces and so forth and then we got a great piece of luck. A twenty-five-roomed house just fell in our lap for the ridiculous sum of £500. It was incredible then, there were news items about it and so on; and we had that house for all the years and were able to develop a business there.

*So you were working together and bringing up your children, when suddenly your husband died. Can you tell me a little bit about the build-up to that, and what happened?*

Well, he became diabetic and he didn't go to a diabetic clinic but it seemed a fairly light diabetes. Then he had a minor car accident and it became worse and then very suddenly he had a small heart attack. And the doctor came to us afterwards and said that he'd have another one and it would be fatal. So in very typical way David said, 'Oh Geoff lays it on a bit thick,' and that was the way he wanted us to take it: you know, pretend it wasn't there.

*So it wasn't discussed as an inevitable thing, but you knew that it was.*

We both knew that it was, yes.

*Did you want to talk about it?*

I wish I'd talked about it in the last day or so because I think he knew that they were the last, but not otherwise. It was his life and he wanted to face it that way, face the end of it that way.

*Do you feel that it was wrong in any way, not to allow you to say things you might have wanted to have said?*

I think perhaps we felt that there was a lot that was tacit between us. I think there is in – not necessarily in long marriages – but in good alliances, there's something tacit that you don't really need to put into words.

*You are very matter-of-fact when you talk now, obviously many years later, about his death and about these practical things. But you wrote a poem called 'Come Away', which won the Cheltenham Poetry Prize, where you talk about the actual moment of death and just afterwards. It is a very passionate poem, full of grief and anger:*

## Come Away

His name
filled my scream
I ran barefoot down the stairs
fast as the childhood dream

when lions follow;
up again I ran,
the stairs a current of air
blew me like thistledown.

I laid my palm on his calf
and it was warm and muscled
and like life.

Come away said the kind doctor.
I left the body there
lying straight, our wide bed
a single bier.

All night I watched
tree branches scratch the sky,
printed another window-frame
for ever on my eye.

When I came home in the morning
all the warmth had gone.
I touched his useless hand.
Where his eyes had shone
behind half-lifted lids were grown
cataracts of stone.

*How did other people treat you? Did you find the world sympathetic in general?*

I had some quite astonishing letters, especially from people we'd done jobs for, because we used to do work mostly in quite large houses in Cornwall. And all these people wrote letters, and an interesting thing is that anybody that had a bill outstanding sent the money almost immediately. I found it such a practical thing, that they did that.

*Did you resent the fact that other men were alive?*

I did resent some other people being alive. I mean, there are some quite dreadful people around that I resented being alive. There was one dreadful farmer's wife who I used to see around the town and every time I saw her I used to think, 'Why should she be walking around?'

*Did anything surprise you about other people? Did David's death bring out things that you didn't expect in people?*

A lot of people would cross to the other side of the road rather than talk, but I think that's quite a common experience; I believe that people feel pretty desperate about it and they wonder how you're feeling and they don't want to speak.

*How did you feel when they did that? Did it make you annoyed or were you relieved?*

I think I just accepted it. I did have a bit of criticism because I didn't have a funeral.

*Well, I was going to ask you that because again in one of the poems you say, 'People said, why did you not follow the coffin?' with a sense that they didn't understand how you were coping with it. Why was that? What was unusual about the way you coped?*

Well I made up my mind about no funeral almost immediately, because he didn't have any religion and often the children would have heard him say, 'When I'm finished you can put me in a brown paper bag,' sort of thing, you know, so I felt that it was the right thing to do. They rang me up from the crematorium and said, 'We have a panel of clergymen, one of them could say a few things,' but they wouldn't have known him, it would have been something by rote. So that's what happened, people have criticized me for this, felt that it was wrong, but I felt that it was right and I still do.

*You personally had no need for ceremony?*

No. The whole thing's so unceremonious really.

*In what way?*

Well, the undertakers come and they just gather the person up and that's it. You know. I suppose if you have a funeral there's all this getting people together. I don't think I'd have liked to have faced that. I mean I went to my parents' cremations and there's everybody standing in that little room and chatting almost jollily really, and then they all go in and the coffin slides away and then they chat jollily again and it seemed to me it wasn't a thing that I wanted . . .

## When You Died

1.

When you died
I went through the rain
Carrying my nightmare
To register the death.

A well-groomed healthy gentleman
Safe within his office
Said – Are you the widow?

Couldn't he have said
Were you his wife?

2.

After the first shock
I found I was
Solidly set in my flesh.
I was an upright central pillar,
The soft flesh melted round me.
My eyes melted
Spilling the inexhaustible essence of sorrow.
The soft flesh of the body
Melted onto chairs and into beds
Dragging its emptiness and pain.

I lodged inside holding myself upright,
Warding off the dreadful deliquescence.

3.

November.
Stooping under muslins
Of grey rain I fingered
Through ribbons of wet grass,
Traced stiff stems down to the wormy earth
And one by one snapped off
The pale surviving flowers; they would ride
With him, lie on the polished plank
Above his breast.

People said – Why do you not
Follow the coffin?
Why do you not
Have any funeral words spoken?
Why not
Send flowers from a shop?

4.
When you died
They burnt you.
They brought home to me
A vase of thin metal;
Inside, a plastic bag
Crammed, full of gritty pieces.
Ground bones, not silky ash.

Where shall I put this substance?
Shall I scatter it
With customary thoughts
Of nature's mystical balance
Among the roses?

Shall I disperse it into the winds
That blow across Cambeake Cliff
Or drop it onto places where you
Lived, worked, were happy?

Finally shall I perhaps keep it
Which after all was you
Quietly on a shelf
And when I follow
My old grit can lie
No matter where with yours
Slowly sinking into the earth together.

5.
When you died
I did not for the moment
Think about myself;
I grieved deeply and purely for your loss,
That you had lost your life.
I grieved bitterly for your mind destroyed,

Your courage thrown away,
Your senses aborted under the amazing skin
No one would ever touch again.

I grieve still
That we'd have grown
Even more deeply close and old together
And now shall not.

*You say your husband didn't have a faith. Do you?*

No.

*After your husband died was there any stage at which you wished you did have a particular religious faith, because it might have brought comfort?*

I might have wished it but I would soon have stopped. Because I feel about death that it's a thing we have to endure, we have to accept it's going to happen and we also have to accept that we don't know if there is anything afterwards; and if there is I don't think it matters that one's paid lip-service to any particular one of these religions.

*You say we have to accept it but people don't, some people fall apart.*

Yes. I think very often it's people who are guilty in some way that fall apart.

*Why guilty?*

Well, because things might have – they might have been kinder, they might have been . . . Within actually about four or five hours of David's death, in the middle of the night, I made a resolution for myself that I would never say 'if only' or anything that sounded at all like 'if only', and I haven't; and I think that's what has made all the difference to how I've managed to conduct the rest of my life.

*Because to look back with regret would have been to spoil what was?*

Yes, it's destructive. I know there are things it would have been better if I had done but I just don't entertain them because it's destructive of the present.

*Let's just talk a little bit about your writing. The fact is that after all those years of working with your husband and devoting everything to family and business, after his death you blossomed into a real poet. You said earlier you had written poetry and he'd written poetry but obviously there was no time to do it. Why did the poetry come then – this real full flowering of poetry? Why after his death?*

I suppose it's the same sort of thing as love, isn't it? It's something that is so strong that it virtually pulls out the stops.

*Grief?*

Yes. I mean, people write poems because they're moved, usually.

*When you were actually writing, was it cathartic for you?*

I do often still weep when I write poetry, so I suppose in a way tears are cathartic, aren't they? I think you have to accept to some degree poems about grief are to relieve yourself but I said this to some person – that I was afraid these poems might be like that – and he said, 'I see them as a celebration of a man,' which I found quite comforting.

*Also they universalize the experience, don't they? Because there could be many widows and indeed widowers and people who've experienced a bereavement who would know exactly what you're talking about in these poems. They're not just about you, are they?*

Well that's what I hope. I do hope that those poems could have a life of their own, it's nothing to do with me. It's like a child that one's had which has grown up.

*What was it like to actually feel that urge again and to actually look at this piece of creation?*

Oh it was wonderful and I was on a real high, sort of drunkenness I suppose, although what I was writing wasn't euphoric by any means. Just the fact that there it was, on paper.

*You said earlier that your husband didn't want to talk about his death approaching and in one of your poems you say that you had 'liberty of speech'. Did you ever wonder when you'd started to write and were getting published, what he would think of it?*

No, that's odd, I didn't. But I did wonder what my mother would have thought of it and perhaps my father.

*Why?*

Well, I think . . . David always expected a lot of me really, expected me to do things well, so he would have just accepted, just taken it as a matter of course. It's odd because I've never thought of that, what he would have thought of them . . .

*Because if he was a reserved man it just occurred to me that he might have – not exactly disapproved – but perhaps wondered about this out-flowing of feeling.*

Yes, it's true.

*Is there any sense in which you were released by the death of your husband into being another sort of person, the sort of woman who suddenly had the confidence to write poetry?*

No, I was more released originally by the marriage. He had a kind of wider intellect than mine and I think I was rather suburban and my mother thought that he put ideas into my head and this wasn't so, it's that my ideas expanded in the marriage. So I think in a way the whole of our working together was an expansion; I think the stage was kind of set really, you know, by the marriage . . .

### Two Years

When you died
All the doors banged shut.

After two years, inch by inch,
They creep open.
Now I can relish
Small encounters,
Encourage
Small flares of desire;
Begin to believe as you did
Things come right.
I tell myself that you
Escaped the slow declension to old age
Leaving me to indulge
This wintry flowering.

But I know
It's not like that at all.

### Four Years

The smell of him went soon
From all his shirts.
I sent them for jumble,
And the sweaters and suits.
The shoes
Held more of him; he was printed
Into his shoes. I did not burn
Or throw or give them away.
Time has denatured them now.

Nothing left.
There will never be
A hair of his in a comb.
But I want to believe
That in the shifting housedust
Minute presences still drift:
An eyelash,
A hard crescent cut from a fingernail,
That sometimes
Between the folds of a curtain
Or the covers of a book
I touch
A flake of his skin.

*You talk very much about the physicality of your husband. Was that very hard to bear, the sense that somebody's body was still actually physically in a house?*

Yes. It is hard to bear. I think that's why I stayed there so long, really. I suppose really you cast it on from your own mind.

*Do you think that's a sort of haunting?*

Yes. I used to feel I could ask him questions and get answers, especially about the business, which he really loved.

*And did you?*

Well, yes I did, yes.

*Did you talk aloud?*

Yes. I didn't actually hear any answers but I felt I got them.

*And you knew what to do?*

I suppose really I knew what to do anyway because we'd worked so closely for so long, but it was a kind of comforting thing to think that there was still a partnership I suppose.

*Over the years your feelings have obviously changed. You said earlier that one has to accept. Are there still times now when you do feel an intense grief and even loneliness?*

Very much, yes. Couples are everywhere, couples are everywhere, walking about, holding hands, you know? You do get hurt by it. You'd be surprised how many people say 'we' all the time: 'we do this', 'we do that'.

*Do your children think you've changed?*

I can't tell really. I mean when you think about it, it must in a way be a kind of relief to have a mother who starts buzzing around all over the place at a late stage in her life and having rewards – not as a poet financial rewards really – but rewards that are perhaps more valuable than financial.

*Certainly to see that you have a new life, yes. Did you ever feel that you might marry again?*

No, I've never wanted to; I've never met anybody I wanted to marry. It wouldn't be a sense of loyalty in that case that deterred me from marriage. If I met someone that I really felt it would be in a way sacrificing my independence for. . . That's what it would boil down to; I can do what I like now.

*And do you really relish that?*

I do except for those moments when you're lonely. One can always feel guilty really about his death having made these things happen, the poetry and things. That might even have happened anyway perhaps. I don't know – but it would have been different of course.

*Although you say very clearly that the poetry did come out of all that was good in your relationship within your marriage, still, is there any sense in which marriage prevented you from having liberty of speech?*

I think the commitment to the work that we were doing meant that I didn't need the liberty of speech. Our conversations would often be about things we were planning. I don't think I consciously ever felt that I didn't have liberty of speech. It's strange how a poem works by itself, how a thing will . . . You suddenly put a thing on paper that you haven't even analysed for yourself. I think when other people sift through your poems they find things that you don't know are there and that's maybe one of them. It doesn't mean that I was gagged, it means that I sort of went outward from that point.

## Coming to Terms

In nearly thirty years he would not say
he loved me. At first I found it hard
having to believe without the words
my upbringing had led me to expect

that he did indeed desire
and need me enough to have gladly
abandoned all others for my sake.
In vulnerable moments I might dare

rashly to ask the forbidden question;
he was adamant, allowing me only
the explanation that, for him,
the word had become debased,

currency of cheap fiction designed
to daze the half-literate. No use
evoking Donne and Shakespeare;
other times, other values.

Growing in love for him, perforce unspoken,
I came to see his reticence as trust,
as tribute to my strength.
The approach of death also

we faced silently, on his terms.
You might say now I have liberty of speech.
Through unshared rooms year after year
I spin words. At first they all

seemed precious, each of intrinsic value.
Now I see they are threads that anyone
may weave; worth's in fine cloth,
a warm coat sewn to fit.

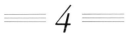

# LORD HAILSHAM

*One of Britain's best-known and respected public figures,*
*Lord Hailsham was the longest-serving Lord Chancellor of*
*this century. His wife Mary died in a riding accident*
*in 1978.*

*In your autobiography,* A Sparrow's Flight, *you've written about your*
*life in a very open way, and you mark it in terms of bereavements. This*
*suggests that the great bereavements that you suffered in your life were as*
*important to you as your achievements. Is that the case?*

I think more important. They were personal. I never regard
myself as having achieved anything. I've lived a very full, varied,
interesting and now very long life, but I don't think of it in terms
of achievement.

*We want to focus on the death of your wife in a riding accident in*
*1978, but before we do that I want to talk a little bit about the other*
*bereavements which may or may not have prepared you for Mary's*
*death. In May 1925 your mother died very suddenly and you write in*
*your autobiography, 'I had no power to make amends.' What did you*
*mean by that?*

In the ordinary course of life one loses one's parents at some time,
but this was prematurely. I feel guilt about all of them, and in the
case of my mother I thought I hadn't been sufficiently open in my
affections. She had of course been very difficult. She'd had – what
I didn't know, although I ought to have known from the

63

information at my disposal – a stroke two years before and she had been very difficult afterwards. I was a young boy of seventeen and I suppose I was a little irritable when she was difficult.

*And so afterwards you felt that you hadn't said the things to her that you should have done?*

Well, I felt about all three bereavements some sense of guilt for quite different reasons and in the case of my mother I thought I'd been impatient with her and not shown the depth of my affection. I have to say about all three that I had never realized the strength of my feelings for any one of them until they'd gone and it was too late to express it.

*Does that awareness have an effect on your behaviour with those who are left?*

Yes, I think it has. I do realize that I might lose other people whom I'm attached to now, and I do try to express myself more openly.

*You mention three bereavements so perhaps we should explain that the second bereavement was in 1932.*

That was terrible of course because my half brother, Edward Marjoribanks, took his own life, and I can't tell you how awful that is when it happens in your family. I've known close friends take their own lives too, so this incident didn't stand alone but it's very much the most poignant as far as I'm concerned.

*You write in your autobiography that it made a permanent mark on you.*

I think it did. It taught me something about taking one's own life which I don't think you can learn in any other way.

*Did you feel that it was essentially a selfish thing to do?*

No, I wouldn't have said that. I have never felt resentment against Edward. He was undergoing a terrible personal crisis but what he didn't realize, and I suppose that nobody realizes who does this awful thing, is the intolerable sense of woe it creates amongst those who love the person. It's something so awful that I can't really find words to describe it.

*But the sense of responsibility is interesting, because you felt that you could have prevented it?*

I could have prevented it, I think. I don't know. He came to me for help and I gave him help. He was eight years older than me and after having taken a doctor's advice I brought him back home to my father and my stepmother and I thought he'd be alright there, and indeed he would have been alright. I told them the doctor had said that he mustn't be left alone, but as I left the house to go about my own business something told me to lock the gun cupboard and I didn't do it. I thought, 'Now don't be silly.' If I'd locked that gun cupboard he might be here today, for what I know. I don't think this was a warning from Heaven or anything miraculous of that kind, but it's something which I did think of and ought to have acted on because it was an extra precaution.

*You write that after your mother's death your father was 'knocked sideways'. Was the extent of his grief a shock to you and did witnessing it enable you to be a little bit stronger, perhaps, when Edward died?*

No, it didn't help me over Edward. It was something quite different. I was profoundly shocked because I was suffering very heavily myself from the loss of my mother, but the sight of my father's grief at the loss of his wife did shake me to the core. Of course I did help him. He wrote to me afterwards thanking me for the help I had given him, but it wasn't enough.

*Did you talk to him about your mother?*

No, not much. It wasn't possible to talk to him about it; for years afterwards, literally years afterwards, one could hear him at night moaning with pain and grief. He didn't know that one could hear him. I was just sorry that I couldn't help about that. I was a little frightened too because when one's revered parent is in this state of mind, it is shocking for a very young person.

*When it came to your father's own death in 1950 you write that he was waiting for the end, desiring it to come because he had been very ill. So when he died were you glad for him?*

I was sorry for myself because life is never the same again after you've lost a parent, but I felt that it was a release for him. He died very peacefully and quietly, knowing that he was going to die; he'd shown immense patience, immense fortitude, in the face of a cruel disability. He had a stroke in 1936 and lived on, paralysed all the way down his right side and unable to speak without hesitation and so on, like all people with strokes. For fourteen years he had to put up with this, and throughout the war when everybody else was doing other things he took the Chair at the Polytechnic Board of Governors. He went to the House of Lords regularly. He chaired committees. All in this state of disability. He couldn't even shave himself properly and he had to have nurses, but he still fought and won.

*I'm interested to find out what you think up to that point you had learnt from the experience of death. I also remember that in the war, for instance, you had to break the news of the death of a beloved only child to a wonderful old man. Did your own experience prepare you better for that?*

I think every experience of pain and grief equips you to some extent to help other people. I've tried to comfort all sorts of people at various times in my life, but the inconsolable relationship is parent and child. It helps in every case that people know you really mind and share their grief, and that you sympathize with them in grief. That is a strengthening factor. But you can't console a parent for the loss of a child, you can only just love them.

*And tell them that you loved the child as well, perhaps?*

Well, in this case he was a very close friend of mine, and I admired him enormously and so did everyone who came into contact with him. He was a very remarkable young man.

*Did you feel as you might also have done when your mother died: why? Did you cry out 'Why?' to the universe?*

No, you can't do that in a war. There but for the grace of God went I. People were dying all around and one couldn't say, 'Why him rather than me?' or, 'Why me rather than him?' or, 'Why this one rather than that?' War is not like that.

*I take that point, but I was thinking of the cry which Lear utters at the end of* King Lear*: 'Why should a horse, a dog, a rat, have life and thou no breath at all?' The sense that perhaps bad men survived and good men died.*

That's what a Greek anthology said: 'War does not spare the good men but the knave.'

*So you accept it as inevitable?*

Well it is inevitable. The bullet has your name on it or it doesn't.

*So we come all the time to fate versus responsibility in a sense, which brings us to the death of your wife. I want to explore both those issues. First could you just tell the story of what happened when you went to Australia in the spring of 1978?*

Well we went there at the invitation of political friends. I had to make a speech at Sydney University, about why a Conservative can be a Democrat and why a Democrat might be a Conservative. It was a political speech, but in the meantime there was a committee of people who had organized this thing and made it pleasant for us. There was one thing they asked me before I went out: 'Is there anything that your wife particularly likes?' And I said, 'Yes, horse riding,' and so she did. She used to ride every week in Richmond Park. It was the thing she liked above all else. And they said they'd arrange a horse riding episode in the tour and so they did, and the only anxiety either of us had was whether with the state of my ankles which was a limiting factor I could ride decently, because I hadn't ridden for some years.

We went round a big park in Sydney called the Centennial Park and we walked for five minutes because of the anxieties about my ankles, and then we trotted for about ten minutes, and I found it was better than I'd expected, and so then my wife said, 'Well, why don't we canter?' She drew away from the rest of us – there were two policemen with us – and I thought she was enjoying herself, and that she'd been bored with the rather controlled way in which I was riding. She disappeared round the bend and suddenly the policeman riding beside me said, 'Which way shall we go?' And I said, 'Go on round the track. That's the way she's gone.' But then I suddenly saw why he'd asked me and I saw what I thought was a stationary car, 'cos even then my eyesight wasn't perfect, and I looked again and saw there was a horse without a rider. And when I got there she was lying in a pool of blood. She'd broken her skull on the back, and I knelt beside her, and she was right out and she never recovered consciousness. At that time I didn't think she was dying. She wasn't dead 'cos I felt her pulse and it was going strongly but she must have died on the way to the hospital. It was a Roman Catholic hospital and nobody dared tell me for a long time. They kept me waiting and these nurses would come in and I would say, 'How is she?' And they said, 'Sister will be here in a moment.' Eventually somebody did come and I said, 'I must know, is my wife alive?' And they said, 'She's dead.' So she was. So then I went in to see her and there was a priest there who was very good.

*You indicate in your book that you felt to blame for her death. Can you tell me why?*

Well, I was to blame for her death in a simple way because as we were packing – we were very short of space – I very nearly said to her, 'Why don't you pack your riding cap?' Which would have saved her you see. Rather like with my brother Edward, this idea had come to me that she ought to take her cap with her and neither of us did pack it. I suppose we could have found room for it, but I didn't force the issue and perhaps I should have done. I was to blame to that extent, but I don't regard it as a great sin or anything.

*There's also, further back in your account, an indication that you almost feel that when you first accepted high office this was preordained, because you wouldn't have been going to Australia. Did you see it as part of a pattern?*

I don't see footprints in the sand in that way. I think there may be a pattern and there have been times in my life when I've thought that I'd traced footprints in the sand, but this wasn't one of those occasions at all. Nobody knows what would have happened to her if she had lived. I've often said to myself since, if she had had a horrible cancer and I'd watched her die slowly it would have been worse for her and perhaps just as bad for me. But there is no answer. It's like what we were talking about in the war.

*You had been married thirty-four years and you describe most movingly your terrible grief at this sudden tragedy. I was wondering, was it worse for you, because you are a very distinguished figure, that your private grief had to be played out in the public eye?*

I don't think anyone avoids it by not being public, because one's life is public to a circle of people. Whether one is working in a factory or practising medicine or whatever, your life is public. The fact that mine was extremely public in the sort of newsworthy sense I don't think enters into it a great deal. Obviously I had to make up my mind about certain things. I could have retired into complete desolation by myself but I deliberately chose the opposite course.

We were then in Opposition and I went and saw Elwyn Jones who was then Lord Chancellor and I said, 'There's one thing you can do for me, and that is to give me some judicial work,' which he did very kindly and I've been grateful to him ever since. And I went and saw Margaret Thatcher and said, 'I'm going to stick it out,' and she understood that too.

I think work is therapeutic. It doesn't soften the pain but it gives you something to do and a sense of purpose and it forces you to face facts of life instead of mouldering away in solitary desolation.

*Thinking back to what you said about your father and his terrible grief, was there any part of you which didn't want to be like that? Which consciously wanted to handle it in a different way?*

I suppose the fact that I had seen the extent of my father's grief made me realize that it was not a wholly uncommon experience, and I've since seen it with wives who've lost their husbands and husbands who've lost their wives. The fact that I'd watched at close quarters somebody else's grief did, I think, enable me, up to a point, to see this thing in proportion.

Two things one's got to remember when one goes through an experience of that kind. One is that the pain at parting is the price you pay for love. It's a terrible high price and the greater the love the greater the pain. But, second, the only way of avoiding that pain would be not to love, and not to share a love and therefore you've got to realize that and be thankful for what you've had which is this thirty-four years of devoted companionship and a common parenthood of charming, delightful children.

You've got to remember that. It doesn't mitigate the pain in any way but it enables you to take a sane view of the situation in which you find yourself.

*What, if anything, gave you consolation?*

I don't think there is any consolation. C.S. Lewis, in *A Grief Observed* describes exactly what I felt. His marriage was a totally different kind of marriage from mine, but he describes this coming up against the brick wall, the complete inability to penetrate the brick wall, and you hammer on the bricks with your fists and nothing happens because there's no way through it. There's nothing more you can say about it; it is a thing with which you either come to terms or you don't come to terms.

*Is it at all helpful to feel that other people out there understand, that they've been through the same thing?*

Yes and no. It is helpful when you get, as my father had got, literally hundreds of letters of sympathy, because it was a very widely publicized event and it was also a somewhat dramatic end. I think that the fact that people wrote so kindly does help. The fact that other people are suffering the same thing may help *you* to console *them* because there are certain things you learn in the course of your experience. One thing you've got to realize is that grief is an illness. It's nothing to be ashamed about; one doesn't want to fight it; tears are a natural safety valve. You don't want to say, 'I'm going to keep a stiff upper lip.' You want to behave with dignity and restraint of course, but it's a great mistake to be ashamed of grief. Nor is there any dividend in it; you've got to suffer it and it's no good trying to pretend that your loved one is hovering somewhere behind your back, wishing you well. You mustn't indulge in fantasies. It is a terrible pain. And it goes on for a terribly long time.

*Isn't there a tendency for people sometimes to feel that, maybe two years have gone, I ought to be over it by now – which is not possible?*

It's possible in one way and not in another. The agony, and it is agony, doesn't last indefinitely. One thing or another may supervene but there's always a scar, and for a very long time – I don't mean a question of two years only, for a *very* long time – there's a dull ache and you wake up in the morning knowing that something is wrong, and you suddenly realize what it is. You're missing them. But the agony does stop within, I should think, twelve months probably. The actual active hideous pain that you suffer does come to an end. It leaves an ache behind.

*You mention C.S. Lewis's book* A Grief Observed *and in it I noticed that he said that he felt a sort of shame when he felt a bit better. Did you have that? Did you feel that it was, in a way, betrayal not to feel the agony?*

Oh no. Oh no. I didn't want to go on feeling the agony. I should have been a masochist if I'd wanted to go on feeling the agony. Nor to be honest would my wife have respected me the better for indulging in grief. One shouldn't indulge in grief. One doesn't have to, God knows, but there's no virtue in feeling pain. It's a thing you feel like toothache.

*Do you think it would be easier to cope with great grief if one did in fact believe in nothing? You write that when your mother died you did not have a faith. Of course, by the time your wife died you'd written a book about your beliefs,* The Door Wherein I Went. *Does that make it harder, because you challenge God?*

I don't think it makes it harder or easier. A lot of people who were believers wrote to me saying, 'Your faith must be a great comfort to you.' Well, I found that it isn't a comfort at all. Faith is not an anaesthetic or an analgesic. You feel just as much pain believing as not believing. The reason one has faith is because of the innate idea, Locke called it, that somewhere the universe makes sense; and your faith is that construct you make round the universe, which is itself a mystery. The Cross wasn't suffered, you know, as a sort of anaesthetic. It was administered without an anaesthetic. That is what unites one to our Lord.

*And the Cross had to be endured by Him. But at the same time He could cry out, 'My God, why hast thou forsaken me?'*

Well He did. Of course one must remember that he was quoting when He did so from the 22nd Psalm and the end of the 22nd Psalm is the Consolation which He received.

*How did you make sense of that suffering – the pain of the Cross – for you personally?*

As one approaches the throne of the mystery one has to express oneself in poetical language. I have, all my adult life from 1940 onwards, occasionally written poetry when I was under stress. On this occasion I wrote two or three poems. I'll read you one of them, if you don't mind; it takes a moment of time. This was written very shortly after the event and this is what it says:

### May 1978

Some Crosses are made of wood and stone
And some of suffering flesh and bone
But all must be carried by each alone
Each to his several Calvary
Crying
*'Eli, Lamà sabachtani'*
Lord why hast thou abandoned me?

My Cross was made of two beams of wood
Between two crucified thieves it stood
And I hung there dying in flesh and blood
On the one and only Calvary
And I cried
*'Eli lamà sabachtani'*
Because I had not abandoned thee

Unworthy of that heavenly food
I stretched my hands for the Body and Blood
Of Him who died on Calvary.
But speak the word I shall be whole,
Sinful body and guilty soul
Oh Thou who died on Calvary,
Never, oh never, abandon me.

*Do you feel that those emotions, the sense that you have not been abandoned, and were never abandoned, can be shared by a person who is now in the acute agony of grief that you described?*

The thing is, this is not the only moment of truth in one's life. The universe is a mystery. Life is a mystery. You either make sense of it or you don't. The choice is between saying, 'It is tale told by an idiot, full of sound and fury, signifying nothing,' or it does make sense.

Now my faith, which is the Christian faith, is the answer to the sense which I can make of it, the best I can do. All religion is basically an attempt to make sense of suffering and wrongdoing and the mystery of this world. The same as science, which is a successful attempt to make sense of the physical universe: what is measurable and what is observable. You don't necessarily have to have faith because you lose your wife, nor does it help you particularly if you do lose your wife to have faith, but if you have got faith you still see the same sense. You say to yourself, you *have* to say to yourself, 'What was true yesterday when I was happy and united is still true now that I am lonely and deprived, just as true as it was when I thought of it yesterday or last week or last month.'

*So you see those deaths and in particular your wife's death as part of a pattern, a design?*

I can't see the footprints in the sand. Sometimes one says, 'This is a punishment; I'm made to suffer this because of what I've done wrong.' But you can't say there's any proof about that, nor is there any necessary connection. My wife died doing the thing she liked and there could only have been one ghastly moment when she went head over heels, but I can't tell what sense there is in that. I can only say that the thing remains a mystery, but I can make sense of life despite that.

*You said before that you didn't think of her hovering behind you, and you used the word 'fantasy' – that one shouldn't see consolation in that sort of fantasy. Yet the essence of the Christian religion is the belief in the Resurrection and the life of the soul. Do you feel that your wife is with you?*

No. I believe in the Communion of Saints whatever that may mean, but there would be neither justice nor mercy in this world if she were not happy where she is.

*Do you think it's true to say that, as far as Christianity is concerned, the meaning of our life is consummated in its ending?*

Well in a sense, yes. It's the one irreversible event in the history of the pilgrimage of the soul. What one does in this life determines the way one goes after it, but nobody *knows* where one does go after it. You can believe in Heaven, as I do, you can believe in Purgatory or Hell, but one knows nothing. One can only believe in the ultimate desire of the soul which is unity with the Godhead.

*Should one make preparation for one's own death?*

Oh yes, I think so. One's under a purely pragmatic duty to dispose of one's possessions by a will. One must try and prepare one's soul for death, which is a very private matter of prayer and a deliberate attempt to come to terms with your sinfulness and to be sorry for what you've done and to try and improve your life such as it remains. You should prepare in practical ways and in spiritual ways.

*And it's like Cicero, quoted by Montaigne: 'to philosophize is to learn to die'?*

This is one of the fundamental questions about philosophy: does life make sense? I remember there was a philosophy don at Oxford when I was there called H.W.B. Joseph who was a logician. He would ask his pupils about cause and effect in science, and the point he was making was this: within us there is that which teaches us that there is sense in what happens: there is a relationship of cause and effect, and there is mind and truth, and I would add, I think above all things, there is *value*. There are value judgements. There is a difference between right and wrong, between good and bad, between kindness and cruelty, and there is a scale of values which has just as much objective reality in the universe as cause and effect or electron and proton.

*It seems to me, reading your book, as if you began life as a rationalist and you've become decreasingly so.*

I think I'm a rationalist now, but I don't think a rationalist needs to be an unbeliever. I think belief is the most rational thing you can do.

*And perhaps it's the supreme act of reason to acknowledge mystery?*

I think it would be insane not to acknowledge mystery!

*Are you afraid of death?*

I'm not afraid of *death* in that sense. All the evidence I have is that it may be a release when it comes. But I'm afraid of dying and I'm afraid of the Judge.

*Why are you afraid?*

Because of what I've done wrong.

*But you believe in mercy?*

Yes, but you've still got to repent. You see, repentance is a much more complex state of mind than people think. It's no good just feeling remorse like poor old Judas. You, you've really got to try and aim at your union with the Godhead, and that you must go on trying to do until the very end.

*Do you think it's important for people to think about death?*

I don't think it's morbid to think about death. People say, 'Don't talk about that, don't be morbid.' It's impossible not to think about death, especially if you're as old as I am, because you know it's coming. And it's just as foolish not to think about death as it is foolish when you're driving not to think about what may be coming round the corner.

*And prepare for it?*

And prepare for it as far as you can, but of course this opens up the whole subject of prayer. I think that the preparation for death very largely consists of learning how to pray.

*But is that ultimately a very lonely feeling?*

I don't think so, but it's a very difficult art. Not one in which I've excelled ever in my life.

*When you were told by the Sister in that hospital that your wife was dead, what was your first response?*

I cried of course, and I said to the Sister, 'We've been married thirty-four years,' and I said, 'I'm sorry,' because one doesn't like to distress other people by signs of one's own grief. But she of course was very kind and understanding and probably knew how to deal with people in this situation.

*And did you pray?*

I asked to go and see her and they sent for – it was a Roman Catholic hospital – they sent for the priest who was on duty and I said to him, 'I must pray,' because he knew of course that I wasn't a member of his church and I don't think he knew whether I had a faith or not. And so there she was lying in front of me on a slab and I did pray, oh yes I did pray. I can remember exactly. I held a sort of little quiet memorial service of my own. I said, 'The souls of the righteous are in the hands of God and no torment touch them though they be punished in the sight of men yet is there hope for their mortality,' and then I broke into the end of the Gloria: Oh Lamb of God that takest away the sins of the world have mercy upon us. Oh Lamb of God that takest away the sins of the world receive our prayer. For thou only art holy. Thou only art Lord. Thou only Oh Christ The Holy Ghost art the utmost high in the Glory of God The Father.

And then I said, 'Grant her eternal rest, O Lord, let light perpetual shine upon her.' And that was it. He said some prayers too. He was a very good priest.

# 5

# ANNA HAYCRAFT
## (Alice Thomas Ellis)

*Writing as Alice Thomas Ellis, Anna Haycraft is a
highly respected literary figure, as well as the mother of five
children. She wrote her second novel,* The Birds of the Air,
*after the accidental death of her son Joshua.*

Joshua was just unbelievably full of life. He used to remind me of
some sort of natural force like a waterfall or a wind or something
like that. It's very, very hard to describe somebody. In all his
photographs he seemed to be bursting out of the picture. He was
always sort of bursting into life and he talked so fast. He talked in
scribble when he was little.

*Lots of energy.*

Enormous energy. And he was very, very loving. He was a very
affectionate, warm, outgoing sort of person.

*Was he naughty?*

He was extremely naughty. He was the naughtiest child I ever
knew. He was always accident prone as well. I remember when he
was two, we were quietly walking along the pavement and he
suddenly leapt into the street and I had to fly out and snatch him
from under the wheels of a passing car. Extremely adventurous
and very funny. Funny little boy, but wild. A wild child, quite
unlike any of my other children.

*Were you very proud of him?*

I adored him, I was extremely proud of him. He was very beautiful. He had fair hair and sort of slanting Slav eyes, lovely bones. I thought he had a sort of genius. He was . . . such life. It was almost a talent.

*He was your second child.*

He was my second child.

*And he died when he was nineteen?*

He was nineteen, yes.

*How did that happen?*

He was discussing with a friend acceleration, and they had a sheet of paper on the kitchen table and they were talking about tortoises and trains, and then they thought they'd go up and watch a train coming out of Euston station and time it. And so they went and sat on a wall near The Edinburgh Castle, a pub, and Joshie had bought a pair of sandals, those biblical sort of ones with just one strap, and he'd said to me, 'Look mum these were only a fiver, weren't they a bargain?' and I said, 'Gosh, yes.' And sitting on this wall one of his sandals slipped off and he went down to get it thinking that the roof beneath was solid. But it was made of asbestos and he went straight through. And he hit himself on the head and then he was in a coma. I think it was eleven months until he died.

*Did you feel that there was something particularly cruel, in that there was a sort of absurdity about that death? Do you understand what I mean when I use that word?*

That was almost exactly what I said to myself: this is preposterous, this is my Joshua, this cannot be happening, it's not true. It's too absurd.

*During the time he was in the coma was there anything that brought you comfort? Could you feel that it might have a happy ending or did you actually know there was no hope?*

I think I always knew he was going to die, but there were certainly very comforting elements in the whole situation. The nurse on his ward was called Sister Lilian, she was South African, and she was an angel. And so I had a sort of revelation of human goodness which I wouldn't have had if Joshie hadn't been there. So that in a way was very comforting.

*Were there other people you met of a similar kind, or other experiences you had during that period?*

All the nurses were good and you know people just were very kind, but there again that was difficult because all the people in the market who'd known Joshie since he was a tiny little boy would say 'How's the boy?' and every time I had to say 'Just the same,' and they were always sort of disappointed. I think everybody was thinking he was going to come out of it, there was going to be a miracle, he was going to be alright. I think I always knew that he wasn't.

*And did you have to go round and tell all those people when he died?*

Yes.

*How did they respond?*

Well I felt so sorry for them because they were so sorry for me and I was so sorry for them being sorry for me. And there again what I should have done was tear down the market, tearing my hair and sobbing, but no, we were all very polite.

*That's an additional burden you had to carry: to make it alright for other people?*

Yes, and to sort of mind my manners. Often I didn't. Well not often but I think twice I screamed and I did find screaming quite good, better than crying. I lost my voice twice after doing that.

*Did you scream in private or did you scream with your husband?*

No, I think I was just sitting at the kitchen table and there were people around and suddenly I thought I've had enough of this – I'd had a few drinks of course by that time – and I just screamed. I gave them a terrible fright, but I felt terribly, terribly sorry for my husband because I kept remembering I had all my children at home and he used to have to fly out and get the gas and air and I just wished I could do something like that for him now. It was even harder for him because men are even less allowed to express their emotions, and he adored Joshua.

*Do you think there is a way in which terrible grief like this can be very isolating: that you can have a married couple each buried in their own grief and they can't reach each other? Was it like that?*

It was very like that. I just felt so sorry for him; there was nothing I could do. I couldn't say, 'It's alright darling, I'm going to make it alright.' But I think that's what we have to do, we have to carry our own grief. I mean you can talk about it but you can't ease another person's burden. They're entitled to it. If it is the thing that makes you grow then you've got to let them carry their share.

*Did you feel at all, either of you, that it might have been the other person's fault? Because there is this need to find a reason?*

Well, I think no matter how a child dies you always have that feeling: I could have done this, I could have said that. I had this

ANNA HAYCRAFT

terrible guilt because the last words I'd said to Joshua were 'Darling, do be quiet,' just before he went out to see the trains, and I'd just been cross with him for feeding all his friends out of the freezer; they'd sort of practically emptied the thing – it was probably tomorrow's lunch they'd eaten or something – so I was cross about that.

*And you told him to be quiet. Do you still think about that?*

Yes. But I think I've forgiven myself to some extent.

*Because I'm sure you think that he's forgiven you.*

He would never bear a grudge, certainly not against me.

*When he actually died, was there any sense in which it was a relief to you that the period of waiting was over?*

I can't say it came as a shock, but again that seemed quite, quite ridiculous. I thought, 'This is not Joshua, not dead, can't be, can't be like that,' and yet it was very curious. It was like being at sea in a terrible storm and then just once or twice as it were the clouds would clear and I'd have this sort of vision of infinite peaceful blue.

*And was that comforting?*

That was very comforting too, yes.

*Where did it come from?*

I don't know; it was almost a physical thing. It was as though I could really see it and with my eyes, not just in my imagination.

*In your novel,* The Birds of the Air, *the main character, Mary, whose*

85

*son Robin has died in a way which is unexplained, is completely
enveloped by grief. Is that how it was?*

That's how it was, yes.

*I don't like asking writers if novels are autobiographical but it seems to
me quite clear that this one did mirror your own experience.*

Yes, it did and I think it helped to write it. Better out than in, as
they say.

*So would you say that producing that novel was in fact something
positive – I hesitate to use the word positive because it's almost crass to
use it in this context, but you know what I mean – something good came
out of the experience?*

Yes, and also I felt that I was writing for Joshua, that I was doing
something that he might have done if he'd lived. I think I carried
on writing with that sort of thing in mind. Sounds crazy doesn't
it?

*So* The Birds of the Air *arising out of Joshua's death was, in a way,
a new flowering.*

Yes.

'Alone in the house Mary stood up. At Melvys y Bwyd a flock
of white geese grazed by a stream where the lane passed
through a farmyard, overhung and dark with trees. She could
see them – so perfectly shaped and delineated that they were
like excisions from some more clearly conceived reality,
making even the barn cats seem amateurly constructed, and
the scuttling and fussing hens bungled – mere mistakes. Then
there was Robin, stencilled against her awareness like the geese
against the Advent darkness, clear and preternaturally real,
quite unlike her tweaked and harassed relations, and shining

always with a radiance that graced the living only when they stood against the snow.

'Well,' she said aloud. She was back in the lane going to the graveyard. It was winter – winter, so there would be berries in the rusted hedgerows, blood-hued from bright scarlet to arterial purple, the fruit of the wild rose and the hawthorn and elder and holly, scattered against the cold sky as though some wounded god running had shaken a bleeding hand in irritable pain. The streams that ran alongside the hedgerows would be frozen to steel and the dead grass stiff with frost. She could feel the wind encircling her head and tears chill on her face.

In the summer there had been no tears. There had been no whipping wind, no onions, no small pains to bring them, and she couldn't weep for Robin – weeping was insufficient and inappropriate. The birds of the air should mourn for Robin and all the vast hordes of the dead.

The sun had shone with great heat for Robin's last day above the earth. It had been a shadowless day without measure so that the flies that rose from the dung heaps in the lane had seemed no less beautiful than the wild flowers strewn under and over the hedgerows. Shy grave diggers, half concealing their rude spades, stood in the rib-high grasses at the unkempt edge of the graveyard, nodding apologetically if they caught anyone's eye.

They had dared to lower Robin in a box into a pit in that dry graveyard filled with sun. It hadn't been then, nor did it seem now, an occasion for tears.'

*One thing I noticed about the character Mary in the novel is that as well as the rage she feels a kind of exultation. That struck me as being extremely interesting because it's something which would surprise a lot of people. It's almost as if the character is in some way defined by death, that – as we've just said about your writing flowering because of it – she is almost finding herself as a person through the experience.*

What I felt, what I tried to make her feel, was simply like a container for grief; that was all that I was; that seemed to be my only point and purpose, just to carry this load around.

*For how long?*

I think it went on for years and I've never felt whole since. I've never felt a complete person. I still feel like a sort of empty thing.

*What affect does that feeling in you have on the rest of your family? Do you think they're aware of that?*

I think they are. I think it makes them rather cross.

*Why cross?*

Because they think I'm not completely there and I'm not paying attention, I'm not giving them quality time, all that sort of thing.

*So there's always a preoccupation?*

Yes.

*You did have another child who died, a daughter, who died at two days old. That was in 1972 before Joshua's death. Did you compare the two feelings? Was there a comparison?*

Well when the baby died I thought nothing could be worse than that and the day she died, Joshua, who was eleven then, came all by himself to the hospital in his little brown gabardine and he cried and cried and cried and I'd said to him, 'It's alright darling, this feeling will go away, you'll feel better about it soon,' and he said, 'Oh I do hope you're right.' The children were terribly upset by that baby's death.

*Did you attempt to talk to them at that stage about death, about the thing that was happening?*

I don't think so, I think I just told them what I actually firmly believe: that people go straight to Heaven.

*So the feeling when he died was of a different quality because you'd known him longer? Is it as simple as that?*

I think it's because I'd known him longer and known him so well and what I found so extraordinary was that every day of his life I'd call upstairs or downstairs, 'Joshua, Joshua' and suddenly I couldn't do that any more. I was never going to say that name again, never call him.

*Did you keep his room as it was? Some people do that, almost making a shrine of somebody's possessions.*

I've kept everything that belonged to him. I tried to fit it all together and put it in a trunk, put it in the attic, but still the house is sort of mined with his things. I pick up a book and open it and it'll say Joshua Haycraft.

*There's obviously a sense of rage that it happened. What I want to know is does the rage change in its quality? It's now twelve years ago; is it different?*

I think that awful burning sensation has gone away. I did feel for a long time as though I was living in the middle of a furnace of pain. It's very very hard to describe because I couldn't have imagined such a sensation if I hadn't felt it and now it's like . . . I suppose if you lose a limb you come to terms with it but it's never going to come back.

*Do you think the outside world actually understands that? Did you feel the world didn't understand you?*

I think so, yes, yes, quite a few of them. Even the children I think were a bit annoyed that their continued existence was not sufficient consolation for me.

*Could you understand that?*

I could see that, yes, yes.

*Do you think there is a terrible pressure on people like you to pull yourself together, to say, 'Life goes on'? That people try and cope with the fact of death in terms of those clichés?*

Yes, I think probably in this country certainly we don't grieve sufficiently when we should. I remember seeing, I think it was some Turkish women at a funeral wailing, swaying from side to side and all one's instincts tell one to do that, but you'd look so stupid wouldn't you, doing it all by yourself?

*Beating your head against the wall?*

That. It was exactly the feeling of tearing your hair, mud and dust to ashes, tearing your clothes, even sort of scratching your face, all those feelings are there and we'd express none of them.

*But are you consciously grieving for Joshua – you said – every day of your life?*

I still miss him every day.

*Do you think about how he would have been now?*

Not very often, no.

*Often people do when they've lost a child, they think each year how old the child would have been and imagine that child changing. But you don't, you've fixed him as he was?*

I think I have a fairly clear vision of him in Heaven and I want to be able to recognize him the minute I get there, so I don't really want him to change.

*I wanted to ask you about faith because you are a Roman Catholic. Was there any time, when Joshua was in his coma and after he died, that you were furious with God, when you railed against God for taking him?*

No, I never got cross with God.

*Why not?*

Well because He'd sent His own son to die that terrible death, it would have been a bit stupid of me to start complaining about mine.

*So therefore the anger was against what?*

The anger was against death. I had a terrific sort of anthropomorphic vision of death.

*As what?*

When we were in the country we kept seeing people with scythes, and I thought, 'There he is, there the brute is.' He was in our lives so much at that time because the year Joshua died two of my friends and I lost twelve people between us, close people. It was rather like living in a mausoleum, you could almost smell the charnel house. I was just so conscious of death, he just seemed like a presence.

*I was interested when I wrote to you and asked you to do this interview: you rang me up and you said, 'There's nothing else to talk about.' Why did you say that?*

Oh dear, well I think because with my closest friends that's what we do talk about most of the time.

*You talk about death.*

Yes.

*Do you still see death personified as the sort of grim reaper figure of medieval iconography?*

Not so strongly as I did. I don't have that sense of almost physical presence any more.

*So you don't see him as threatening?*

No, and I don't think he's hostile, I think he's just there.

*And is there comfort in talking about it, or isn't that what's sought?*

No I don't think that's the point of it. It's just that it's there.

*So you're just contemplating it and acknowledging it.*

Yes, trying to understand.

*Is there a growth in this process?*

I'm not sure. I think it's just an absolute sort of ongoing thing, just carry on crawling round and creeping up on it and having another look. But it just crops up all the time.

*Could you extract any meaning from all those events?*

I think I just went absolutely into automatic, and it had to be faith and I had to believe that it would be alright. A friend of mine recently lost her son and I said, 'It's alright, you've got to believe it's alright,' and I firmly believe that. It is alright. You can't understand it now, you can't see the purpose of the pattern but I somehow know it's alright.

*Someone like me who doesn't have that faith finds it enviable, because I can't imagine ever seeing anybody I have lost ever again.*

You will.

*It would be very interesting to know why you're so convinced of it, because faith is tested every day, and something like the death of a child must test faith more than perhaps any other experience. What is it that enables you to believe with even more conviction than ever?*

Well it's partly I think because I believe in order, and if I had lost Joshua for ever then it would be nonsense, everything would be completely nonsensical: there'd be no point or purpose, no meaning, no order.

*If you look back now at that time, at his death, are there any things that you wish you'd had from other people that you didn't have then? Do you think people could have handled it better?*

No I don't think so. There was nothing anybody could have done, there was no consolation to be had from other people at all, nothing, nothing, nothing. The only – consolation isn't the word, but this is why we talk about it all the time – it's the sort of shared experience and it's like talking to somebody who's been to the same country as you've been to. If they haven't you can't discuss it.

*So you think people can't even make the imaginative leap?*

I don't think so. Unless you've gone through it you can't imagine what it's like. You think you can but you can't.

*You said earlier that Joshua was a very funny, humorous person. After he died were there any incidents which had the kind of black humour we associate with your books, that he might have thought funny?*

Well, I thought all the time that he was probably conscious of what was going on. What I mostly felt was that he wouldn't like me to be too unhappy, and I had conversations with him: 'It's all very fine and logical for you, darling, you're alright, but you've left me.'

He came back to me in a dream twice and the first time he was better; he wasn't completely well, but he was definitely on the mend and he said to me, 'Mum, you've got to realize this is the worst thing that's ever happened to you,' and I said, 'Darling, you didn't have to come back and tell me that.' And I thought later what he meant was that this is the worst, nothing worse can happen, that's it, it's over, whatever happens next may be as bad but nothing could be worse. And then another time I had a different sort of dream, I was in the country and he had come back and I said, 'Joshie, you have given me such a fright, do you realize I've had a tombstone put up for you and do you understand what it costs? Somebody's going to have to pay for this!' And I had such an overwhelming sense of relief: 'Oh you're home, you're back.' And then I woke up and it took me – I could see the leaves blowing outside the window – it took me a couple of minutes to realize that it was only a dream.

*And was that a terrible waking?*

No, in a way the feeling had been so strong that he was still alive, and as I keep saying, it's alright. Again that was a sort of consolation.

*And did you feel – do you feel – that he was actually bringing you comfort?*

I think so, yes. I think he'd been permitted, I think he'd been let, you know, just that brief tiny little second, to remind me that he was alright.

*So that's like a visitation.*

A bit like that, but it's that curious thing about dreams because Gerald Welles said, 'dreams are like rumours, some you must believe and some can be discounted as absolute rubbish', and those were true dreams I think. They were two true dreams. Different in kind.

*But you believe them?*

I believe them.

# 6

# VAL HAZEL

*Val Hazel is a kindergarten teacher from Brentwood in Essex.*
*Her son Geoff died of a brain tumour.*

We were quite an ordinary family. We lived in Essex in a chalet
bungalow. John and I decided when we were first married that we
wanted a large family, we wanted four. Unfortunately our first
little girl died shortly after birth and we were dreadfully upset
obviously and when I became pregnant with Geoffrey I was very
worried about this. But he was born very easily and we were
overjoyed that we had, as we thought, a very healthy child. And
he was followed a couple of years later by Dena and a couple of
years later by Sasha. So there we were: we had our son and our two
daughters and we were absolutely content. We thought we really
had the world in our hands. It was wonderful. They were good
children and they had lots of friends. The house always seemed to
be full of children, and trikes, and sandpits and goodness knows
what else. Yes, we were very, very happy. I think we probably
gave our lives over to the children. We felt that it was important
that they had a happy life. I was an only child and I was giving
them things that I had longed for: the companionship of other
people. John was at the time working in local government, and I
was just a housewife at home looking after the children – which I
thoroughly enjoyed.

*When did you first know about Geoff's condition?*

When he was about nine or ten months old he began to have a form of fit and he was taken into hospital and they investigated. They couldn't really find anything wrong, and this went on: they gave him steroids and these stopped the fits, and this life went on for several years. Then he began to have fits again, and we took him back to the hospital, and eventually he went into St Bartholemew's Hospital and they found there that he had a cyst on the brain. They operated on that, and then about eight or nine months later they found that he also had a rare tumour. Apparently they were unconnected, which I've always found very, very difficult to believe, and I think the tumour was discovered when he was about six and a half – that was when he was in Bart's. By then we'd been transferred to a cancer ward where they were absolutely marvellous and we had the support of not just the staff, but other parents who were in the ward at the same time.

*And what was the prognosis?*

At that time we were told it was a very serious and rare cancer, and they told us in a very, very positive way that he had at least a thirty per cent chance. And we thought, 'Oh, thirty per cent,' and then of course you realize that in actual fact it's a seventy per cent chance against. But he pulled through. His weight went down at one point to just under two stone and they gave him steroids again and he began to eat and he really came on marvellously. He came home and seemed very fit and well and we heard about a charity that was being set up which was aiming to give holidays to chronically sick and terminally ill children. They were taking them on cruises. I got in touch with these people and as they hadn't really had a chance to think it through Geoffrey became the figurehead. They actually called it the Geoffrey Hazel Fund, and we took lots of children on holidays.

*Well at this stage you were very much facing out to the world, as well as looking into your own problems, but did you know then that Geoff was actually going to die?*

They were always very, very hopeful at the hospital but I think I knew deep down that we didn't have long with him. I'm sure that I couldn't see him growing up. I couldn't see him starting work. I couldn't see him married with a family.

To all intents and purposes he was cured. He went back to school, but that wasn't a great success because he couldn't see out of one eye; so they transferred him to a school for handicapped children, but he wasn't happy there, and that really was when he began to go downhill. That was in 1976, and he was eight.

*When did it become clear to you that you didn't have very long with him? When did they actually tell you?*

We'd taken him to hospital again, and they did another brain scan, and they said that the tumour had regrown and that was when they told us that he would have about three months.

*What was your first response to that?*

An agony that I couldn't go with him. I think this upset me more than anything: the fact that he had to make this journey on his own, whereas I'd been with him for all his hospital appointments. I really wanted to be with him, but in a way it was very, very strange because my mother had died when I was twenty and then we'd lost our first baby about four or five years later, and with my mother I had the dream many, many times that she had died and she'd come back to us just for a few months. And then when we lost the baby I had the same dream about her, and when Geoff came home it was very much as though I was reliving that dream. It had been a horrible dream; I'd woken up, I'd cried, and it had hung around for several days, but when he came home I think that dream helped me. I'd been there before. I was able to plan all sorts of things and I discussed them with John, because I was worried that after Geoff died I might not be able to cope, and I thought, 'If I can't cope then the family collapses.' So I began to plan what I would do. We had a very good curate who would come round to see Geoff, and I asked him if he would take Geoff's funeral service and he said he would. I began to plan the funeral. I didn't see this as giving up. I saw this as accepting things and any tribute that we paid to Geoff after his death was very very important to me – almost like you would give someone a good wedding. It was the last thing that I could possibly do.

*Was he aware when all this was going on that he was going to die? Did you tell him?*

No, I didn't. The modern thought is that you discuss with the child the fact that they are going to die, but I didn't feel I could do that because at that time he was nine; now if he hadn't been able to accept it, what could I have done? I couldn't help him.

*Did you tell your daughters?*

No, no. I thought they probably had guessed but they didn't. They would still talk about when he got better. It was just a time of limbo really. He was ill, and we were nursing him, and they'd been so used to him being ill I think they thought he eventually would get better.

*How did other people respond to you?*

Ah. I had to go out and make people respond because other people were aware of what was happening, and we had Geoff in a wheelchair, and people were quite happy to say, 'Oh hello, good morning,' and scurry past, and I didn't want that. I wanted him to have lots of friends around him, so I would go up to them and I would talk to them, and I would explain how Geoff was, and he would talk to them. His voice was very slurred lots of the time, but he would talk to them. I was trying to educate them in one way. I was very, very hurt by a neighbour when I asked her to come in, and she said, 'Oh no, I don't want to come in and see him; I'd rather remember him as he was.' And he didn't look particularly thin. He didn't look particularly ill. It's just that this awful thing was going to happen to him. That I found very hard to bear.

*As Geoff deteriorated were you afraid at all of the effect it would have on your daughters?*

Very much so. At one point we discussed this, and we decided that as much as we wanted him to die at home, if it had a bad effect on the girls then he would have to go into hospital, purely because of the fact that they had the rest of their lives to lead and we didn't want anything to spoil that. But it just happened so naturally and peacefully and we were so very, very, very glad it did. We were – it sounds funny to say lucky – but we were lucky. I do use that word. I've heard of other children, the way they've died, and I think we were extremely fortunate.

*Why?*

Well he just closed his eyes and died. I'd heard of children having haemorrhages and all sorts of things, but he literally closed his eyes and went to sleep. It made sense of the phrase 'they fell asleep'. I was sitting holding his hand. When we looked at him, his lips were turning blue and so were his nail beds and I just sat by the bed and held his hand and my husband was by my side. The girls were upstairs and he just closed his eyes and that was it. He just slipped away very, very quietly, very peacefully. There was no fear, no anxiety. It was beautiful. It was something that I've been very, very thankful for.

*And what about your daughters? How did you tell them?*

Well, we went upstairs. They were up in their bedroom and we went up and told them, and Dena shrieked and we took them one on each knee and talked to them gently. I said, 'Look, Geoff's downstairs, he looks perfectly happy, he looks as though he's asleep. Would you like to come and see him?' And they said, 'No, no, we don't want to.' I said, 'Well, don't you think you might be glad if you did because he really does look as though he's asleep?' And they said, 'Yes, alright.' So we carried them downstairs and they couldn't believe it. And I said, 'Come on, he needs washing now. Will you help me get a bowl and some soap and a towel and we'll wash him?' And we just washed him very gently and they were in and out of the room and they were quite happy. I think the way we handled it was purely by instinct and it could have gone horrendously wrong. It could have been something that frightened them enormously but in actual fact I think it has helped them very much, because I don't think either of them are frightened of death. Dena has now gone on to nurse; she's obviously seen death again. I think the peace of that morning has stayed with them for the rest of their lives.

*Did they want to know where he'd gone? Was there that level of questioning?*

I did find that rather difficult to handle, but his grandfather had died a couple of months before and they knew that my mother had died, and I said, 'Well, he's gone to be with Nanny and Grandad,' and they could accept that.

*And had you brought them up to believe in Heaven, in life after death?*

Yes. We didn't go to Church at that time, but I would say that we were a Christian family. We would go to church on rare occasions and in those days they had assemblies and Religious Education at school, so they were very much aware of the fact there was a God and a Heaven. We told them that Geoffrey didn't have any pain and that he'd had so much pain and really couldn't bear any more and this was what had been taken away from him. They could identify with the fact that God had taken him because he was too sick to live.

*Did you ever think that a child dying was something that shouldn't happen?*

Do you mean did I ever say, 'Why me?'

*Yes.*

No, because if you say that, in effect you're saying, 'Well why should it be me? Why shouldn't it be the person down the road?' But I turned it round and I thought, 'Why shouldn't it be me?' I'd done nothing wonderful in my life to prevent anything bad happening to me or to Geoff. I felt it was a very negative attitude, wishing in a way it had to happen to someone else. And that wasn't fair, I mean that person probably wouldn't have done anything bad to deserve it. I've learnt since that there are lots of people who have had that attitude and it has made them bitter. I'm not saying my family didn't have that attitude: the other members would say, 'Why him, he's only little, he's never done anyone any harm.' But I didn't have time for that.

*But for those who seek acceptance in the face of death, the acceptance of the death of a child is perhaps the hardest, isn't it? If it's an older person you can say they had a full life . . .*

I did feel that when other people lost their husbands or wives at perhaps sixty, seventy, and they were saying, 'Why me? Why did it have to be him?' My immediate reaction was, 'But my Geoff only had ten years; he had sixty years more than Geoff.' Then I would begin to feel bitterness creeping in . . .

*You said that planning Geoff's funeral was very important to you; did it work out as you'd planned?*

It was a wonderful day. Again that sounds odd, but I think having spoken to the curate about it, he must have gone away and planned it himself, and he was wonderful. He wrote a marvellous sermon about three trees on a hillside and the trees hadn't wanted to be on the hillside, they'd wanted to do various things, and one of the trees had wanted to point the way to Christ and of course they ended up using that tree as the Cross. So the tree had its wish in the end. And the point of it was perhaps Geoff's life *has* led to something, although we think it's been cut short and he hasn't achieved anything, in lots of ways he has achieved lots more than other people will ever achieve in the world, partly because of the fund that was named after him. He's helped so many people and his death was not useless.

It was a lovely funeral, very beautiful. We chose his favourite hymns. We had 'All Things Bright and Beautiful' and 'Lord of All Hopefulness' because above all I wanted people to think of things as being hopeful. I didn't want them to think that death was the end and I didn't want anyone wearing black. Unfortunately people thought that was being a little bit disrespectful and they did turn up in black but I would have had everyone in the brightest of colours, because he didn't understand black. He would never have understood why people were wearing black. His attitude would have been, 'Well I'm not suffering any more, Mum, so you should be wearing bright colours.'

Also, we'd planned what we would have on his headstone because when he was about three my husband went into him very early one morning and Geoff said, 'Is it time to get up Daddy?' and John said, 'No, Geoff it's only dawn,' and he said, 'Oh, I know what dawn is: it's when the sun comes up and dries up all the dark.' And we thought about this and we thought what a marvellous thing to put on his headstone. For him the sun had come up and dried up all the dark. The dark being the pain and his actual death the dawn, with the sun coming out. And we've got a sun on his headstone, a bright sun, and his words actually written on the headstone which cheers me up enormously every time I go there. Funnily, I noticed that in our local paper someone used that phrase for someone else who had died. They must have seen the words on his headstone, and taken them away and used them when a relative of their's had died. So it's done a little bit of good.

*What was the attitude of people you knew, after the funeral?*

I think they were looking for my second head. They would look at me as much as to say, 'Well, why are you walking around? You should be at home grieving.' It was most peculiar: you could see this look flash into their eyes before you actually said anything, and I would have to go up to them and say, 'Hello, how are you?' Then they would mumble something like, 'I'm very, very sorry,' but I know people were trying to avoid me and I didn't want that. I wanted to be treated as though I was perfectly normal but people are very, very worried about whether they're going to make you cry. They don't realize that crying is a very healthy part of grief. They really looked at me in a most peculiar way. Perhaps I'm imagining it, but I don't think I am.

*Did you want to talk about Geoff?*

Oh endlessly, absolutely endlessly, yes. I found this was fine because being in Bart's we were all in the same boat. We supported each other and when Geoff was dying there must have been a child who died every two or three weeks, and I was in touch with all the parents and we rang each other, and we were just talking about the children endlessly. And it wasn't all doom and gloom: we were laughing about some of the tricks they used to get up to in the hospital and it was a tremendous source of help. I've always found that people who have been through it can help far more even than members of the family. They know exactly what you're feeling, exactly whether you want to be left alone or whether you don't. That's fifteen years ago, and I'm still in touch with – must be eight or nine of them now. Perhaps it's dwindled down to Christmas cards but if we do see each other or we speak on the telephone we can still pick up exactly where we left off.

*So there's a sense in which Geoff's illness and death put you in touch with a larger world, isn't there?*

Oh definitely, absolutely definitely, yes.

*You said earlier that it was very important for you to plan, because you knew that if you fell apart, the family would fall apart. Were there ever times when you thought, 'Well, I've been strong but I need to be weak now'?*

I think underneath it all I felt weak the whole time. But I'm one of those people who puts a face on it anyway; whatever happens I probably won't let people know how I really feel. John would be the only one that I would talk to and we would get upset together then. He especially found it very difficult because he didn't have the chance to talk to people the way I did and he's a very quiet person anyway, who does hide his feelings. I think he found it extremely difficult not being able to let go.

*Was there a particular pain too in the fact that this was your only son?*

Certainly for John there was, because he'd lost his father just two months before Geoff died and then he lost Geoff and he said he felt as though he was part of a chain and suddenly both links had been broken and he was there on his own. I don't know whether I noticed it more being a son – I think possibly I did – but then again if I'd lost one of the girls I don't think it would have been any easier.

*After Geoff died did you have any strong desire to make up for him? You'd said you wanted a large family . . .*

We thought about having another baby and we hummed and hawed; we couldn't really make up our minds. I didn't want to replace Geoff because I knew that was absolutely impossible, but

I did want to give the family something else because I felt that if we had something positive to look forward to then it would help us all. In the end we decided to and I was lucky: I became pregnant immediately after we'd made the decision. So another sister was born on Christmas Day, eighteen months after he died. The previous Christmas was the first Christmas spent without Geoff and we were determined it was going to be absolutely wonderful for the girls: they weren't going to suffer in any way because we'd lost Geoff. We knew we would be sad and I remember saying to John, 'It's not so bad, is it?' and bursting into tears. I thought I couldn't go through another Christmas like that. But Anna was born on Christmas Day, which was something I felt was *meant*. That's given us a whole new meaning to Christmas. Probably all our Christmases we would have been aware of the fact that Geoff had died, whereas now the focal point of Christmas is the fact that it's Anna's birthday as well, and this has helped enormously.

*What do you think the long-term effects were on your daughters?*

From the time Geoff was in hospital Dena wanted to nurse and we thought it was something that she would probably change her mind about, but she didn't. When he was actually home she was very, very good. If he wanted to go to the toilet and I was upstairs (he couldn't walk by this time) she would go and get his bottle and unzip his trousers and see to him. Then she would say to me, 'It's alright Mum, I've done it all.' She wasn't even eight at that time. So I thought it was wonderful she wanted to be a nurse, but we wondered whether she was doing it for us, because we felt that perhaps she thought that's what we would have liked. We did urge her to think of other careers, but she was adamant she was going to Bart's. Anyway, in the end she was accepted at several hospitals and she did choose to go to Bart's. She didn't mention to anyone that she'd had a brother there and when she was in her second year she was asked to go on to Geoffrey's ward: the children's cancer ward. They were having some introductory lectures before she went on the ward, and there was a film about children with cancer and she broke down in the middle of the film, and they asked her why, and she said, 'Because my brother died; he was on Kenton Ward.' They said, 'Really, we think it's wrong for you to nurse on this ward, you can go on to the other children's ward.'

Well it happened to be Christmas and, of course, the two wards were amalgamated and in the end she was given a three-year-old boy with leukaemia to look after, and she loved it. They were very, very impressed with her and asked her to consider going back there when she finished training, but in the end, just before she finished, she ended up on the Neurosurgical ward, which was another one of Geoffrey's wards. This is a very high-tech ward. She's not very keen on just ordinary nursing; she likes something where there's a challenge, and of course there was a challenge on W.G. Grace Ward. When she passed her Finals and had to look for a job as a staff nurse, there were two jobs going on W.G. Grace and she applied and got one.

She's been there ever since and enjoys it very much, but she was very upset a few weeks ago. There was a girl dying with a similar tumour to Geoff and Dena identified very much with the family. She wanted to say something to them, but didn't want to give them any negative ideas because Geoff had died. In the end the child did die and Dena, I think, was a bit of a comfort. She went to the funeral and tried to support the mother as much as she could. I think Geoff's death helped her in that, because she knew how they were feeling.

She feels, in fact we all feel, that we've perhaps acquired another sense with having had Geoff: you're more perceptive really. You're more aware of other people's needs. People I speak to, particularly friends I've known since Geoff – if they haven't had a tragedy in their lives, there is something missing. That sounds awful, but when you have a tragedy it seems to give you an awareness of other people's needs. And other people don't always have this. So there aren't always negative aspects to tragedies.

*Do you think Geoff himself had that other sense?*

Without a doubt. In fact I almost feel that he was born with it. Whether his life was planned before he was born I don't know. Some people would say that it was. I can remember, on lots of occasions, people would perhaps have a cold, and then Geoff would say, 'Oh I'm sorry you've got a cold,' and we wouldn't see them for ages afterwards, and then they would come round or we would go there and he'd say, 'How's your cold?' He was always aware of their needs and the fact that they hadn't been well. He would remember all the little things about them. He really was a super little lad.

*Do you think about him a lot?*

All the time, constantly, yes. His photo is – well, we've got lots of photos in the house but one of them's in the sitting room and I often say, 'Night, Geoff' or 'Hi, Geoff' as we go in and if we're going on holiday and no one is going to be in the house then I'll always take the photograph with me. But if one of the girls is going to be in the house then I leave the photograph for him to look after them. It's most odd.

*Perhaps you don't want to leave him on his own?*

Yes, I wouldn't want to leave him on his own but it's mainly that I wouldn't want the girls to be on their own, without his photograph there.

*Do you think it's important to tell people who are bereaved that in fact, to use that overused phrase, you* never *'get over it'?*

I think so, because sometimes people ring me and say, 'It's been two years and I don't feel any better,' and I say, 'It's something you've got to learn to live with. It's not something you will ever get over. You will learn to live with it. You will learn that the happier times are more important.' I have to think hard now to think about the awful times, and there were many, many awful times: waiting for results of tests and when they come they aren't what you want and you're living in a constant state of anxiety . . . Well, that's gone and now I remember the happy times. I just feel very, very happy that we were the ones who had him and I don't envy anyone. In fact, I suppose, I feel a little bit sorry for people that they didn't have Geoff as their son, you know? I'm the lucky one, even though he's gone. I had him just for ten years and I think we all feel that he enriched our lives so much that the suffering we've gone through since has been very well worth it, it really has. I would go through this suffering a thousand times more just to have had him for those ten years because it – it was just marvellous. I feel very privileged that he was our son.

*Geoff died fifteen years ago; is that as fresh to you, in that you still need to talk about him?*

I don't think that that need will ever, ever diminish. I thoroughly enjoy talking about him because it brings him back for a short time, and I find that I like to be with people who've known him because any naughty things that he's done, we can laugh about. I don't ever want to be gloomy, because he wasn't a gloomy person. He was a happy person, in spite of everything. But I do find it very difficult when people I'm meeting for the first time ask, 'How many children have you got?'. I find I have to say, 'I have got three daughters, and I had a son who died of cancer.' I can't deny Geoff at all. My reasoning is that if he lived in Australia I would mention it and because he's moved a little bit further on I see no reason why I shouldn't bring him into the conversation. Of course, in Victorian times they would always say, 'I've got three children and two in the churchyard,' and that is such a natural way. I've never actually used it because I think it might shock people, but I do feel like saying that: 'I have three daughters and a son in the churchyard.'

*People don't understand, do they, that the person is always beside you?*

Yes, yes. The funny thing is, the girls and I are untidy and if we lose anything we say, 'Geoff, come on, help us, where is it?' because he was so tidy. And we always find it. I presume it's just coincidence.

*You have a strong sense of his presence; is it at the age he was, or the age he would be now?*

I think I see him as he was. I don't think I see him as a twenty-five year old. Sometimes I wonder what he's like, and I have to be honest, I don't really like seeing his friends because then I begin to think, 'If only.' If you go down that road then it does become very gloomy, so I prefer not to think about that. I like to keep him as a young lad. As someone said to me once, 'The thing is, he will always be yours.' That's absolutely true; because he was taken from us at such an early age, he's remained ours. He hasn't got married and gone away. He's always stayed our son, and closer to us than anything. It's a very selfish way of looking at it – but it's something that does . . . that does help.

$$=== 7 ===$$

# BERNARD LEVIN

*The* Times *columnist, author, and television journalist
Bernard Levin remembers his friendship with the novelist and
journalist Peter Forster.*

*Is it possible for you to define friendship?*

I don't think I can define it. I think I can say what it has meant to
me and it has been – I'm in no doubt at all of this – the most
important thing in my life. I have never married and friendship
has been – not a substitute for marriage and a family – but a kind
of parallel running alongside it, and I'm only on one side of the
road. And my friends have been to me the mainstay of my life,
not just in the obvious ways in which I love my friends and they
me and we meet and we talk and we feed each other and all those
things which are very important, but they've given me a kind of
anchor for my life that I would otherwise not have had, the kind
most people have in marriage and families, or those who have a
religious faith. I have neither of those, except the second, in a very
amorphous way. They've given me – I don't think it's exaggerat-
ing to say – they've given me a meaning for my life that I
otherwise would not have had.

*When did your friendship with Peter Forster begin?*

Many, many, many years ago. I think the first time I met him was
when he lived in a block of flats where an even older friend of my

youth lived. That must have been thirty years ago or thereabouts.

*What kind of man was he?*

I have to start by saying he wasn't the same man all along, but when I first knew him he thought – and then there was good reason for him to think – that he was going to have a huge success in life. And he was very breezy, he was very funny, he was a very witty man to the end of his life; a very witty man and a very ebullient man and one who barged through life in a rather engaging manner. I took to him immediately and him to me though we were very different kind of people. And he was convinced, absolutely convinced, that he was going to make a success and indeed he once buttoned-holed James Eggart. Eggart was perhaps the most famous theatre critic Britain has ever had. When he, Peter, was little more than out of his teens and I suppose he'd just been to university, he bearded Eggart in the Café Royale where Eggart used to hold court, tapped him on the shoulder and said, 'Mr Eggart, I intend to succeed you in your job as the theatre critic of the *Sunday Times*.' And Eggart, who was always good at that kind of thing said, 'Sit down and have some champagne, you silly boy,' and talked to him. But that was exactly how to define him, because it wasn't just sport and he did say to himself, 'I'm damn well going to have that job.' He didn't quite get it, incidentally, but he did flourish early. He got some very good jobs and was really making a name for himself.

*Did you quarrel with him ever?*

Not until the bad end, no. He was a very touchy man . . .

*. . . a difficult man?*

He was a difficult man. He became more difficult. When he was younger he was brash and ebullient and outgoing and so he was for the rest of his life; but he was touchy and that was difficult, but not in any very serious way. We never had a quarrel; we might shout at each other but we never even remotely got close to breaking the friendship.

*He was a well-known journalist and wrote a good many novels. That was what he wanted to do, wasn't it? He really wanted success as a novelist.*

He wanted success as a novelist and he wanted success very, very badly indeed. What began to destroy his life was the fact that although his books were published – and on the whole certainly his first book *The Primrose Path* was very well received – they didn't sell. You know how many novels are published every week and why this one succeeds and why this one doesn't succeed nobody will ever say. So *The Primrose Path* was a good book, it was well received, but it only made a very modest sale and he was very, very disappointed. He got over that, but then it happened again and again. All his books published to some acclaim but none of them made a success as far as sales were concerned. And the great blow was when his publisher went to another publishing house to a more senior position. Peter sent him his next book saying, 'Well, you're now the boss, or one of the bosses, and here I am with my next novel,' and the publisher wrote back and said, 'I'm very sorry I can't publish it,' implying, though not saying, that it wasn't good enough. And that was a very, very, very bitter blow because all his books had been published, not successfully as I say, but they had been and this was actually turned down and by the man who had worked with him for so long.

*Did he talk to you about the disappointment?*

Yes, he did and that was the beginning, I think, (though I can't quite remember the chronology of it all), of the deterioration. Because he was a vain man – well, who am I to talk? I'm an extremely vain man – but he was a vain man and he really thought that he deserved the success. Actually he did deserve the success, obviously because he was a good writer and a good novelist; and you couldn't tell him, 'Look it's a lottery, you put a ball on the spinning roulette wheel and it falls into this or that number and there's no justice in it.' That's all true, and I told him so many times but he wouldn't listen. He wanted success and he thought he deserved it. One phrase of his sticks in my mind – I think it was about the last book of his that got published. There were a few paragraphs in the reviews commending him but nothing much, and he said, 'This time, this time, I thought they would come out with their hands up.' And it was no good telling him that they don't come out – Anita Brookner or Anthony Burgess or whoever you are – it's not a matter of quality or at least it's not a matter *only* of quality. The whole damn thing's a lottery. Thank God I've never written a novel or wanted to. And that really began to sour his life.

*With what effect?*

Two things. First of all his marriage broke up. Then he married – no he didn't marry, they lived together – a marvellous, marvellous, wonderful woman, a very, very beloved friend of mine to this day and to the day of my death, and they lived in France and that's when it really began to go wrong because she was – I won't say steadfast – she was like a thousand steadfast angels. But his life became sour and, alas as does happen, he took to drink and it got on top of him, it got on top of him in a very large way. And finally this marriage, or quasi-marriage, broke up, and they parted and then Peter came back to Britain to try to make another career. Then he became, in the old phrase, 'his own worst enemy' because apart from the drink itself – which at that time was getting on top of him but had not got on top of him – he did himself in, in a sense. You know, it's like the man throwing the lifebelt overboard before the ship sinks. He wanted jobs, he wanted journalist's work, got some and then quarrelled. He became a quarrelsome man. *We* didn't quarrel, at least not seriously quarrel, but he became a quarrelsome man from sheer disappointment. His life was a disappointment. Everybody's life is a disappointment. I suspect Beethoven thought his life was a disappointment, if you really got down to it. I think my life has been a disappointment. But Peter allowed that to get on top of him and he became a very embittered man because he thought, I think rightly, that he was good enough to make a real success and he didn't. And then he began to deteriorate under the effect of the drink. I've known heavy drinkers and people who've got drunk, but he's the only one in my life that I can think of who really destroyed himself with drink.

*Quite deliberately, do you think?*

Well, of course it's deliberate isn't it? It's a kind of protracted suicide. God knows, it must be the worst suicide in the world. I mean you get a gun and shoot yourself in the head or take an overdose of sleeping pills and that's it, that's a moment, but this was a hideous, protracted death. Now I don't really understand the etiology and God knows I don't want to be an amateur psychoanalyst here, but there must be some self-destructive urge in someone who gets on to drink or drugs. Of course these days much more. Why people want to destroy themselves with these things, I don't know, and why they want to do it in so hideous a way is even more of a puzzle to me, but Peter did, and he became really quite unbearable at times when he was in the drink. But the tragedy of it, a deeper tragedy, is when we met and he wasn't actually drunk or he was at a good patch in between, he was the man we knew before. He was warm and funny and made wonderful jokes and witticisms and talked well, he talked very well indeed, and we would have lunch or something. Then three days later he was in one of his fits and it was all bad again. He tried several cures. There's a pill you take that if you drink you get violently sick so you don't drink, but of course what you do if you're a real drunk is stop taking the pill and that's exactly what he did. Then I got him into a place with an enormous record of success, a huge, amazing record of success; it was called Broadway Lodge in Weston-Super-Mare, and I knew about it because a friend of mine had been through it and had survived it and got cured. So I persuaded Peter to go there. He was in hospital with a suspected heart attack and that really had frightened the wits out of him because the doctors said, 'This isn't a heart attack but if you go on drinking like this you'll kill yourself, and that's that.' And that really frightened him, and I got him out of the hospital and into Broadway Lodge. But he didn't stay there. He fled it after a week, cursing them. I have to say the reason was that they demand a great deal of the people who go there. They demand a great deal of intensive work and above all – this was the thing – they make them face reality. You can't do anything else. But Peter didn't want to face reality, simply didn't want to face reality because it was too painful. I can understand that; it would have been very, very painful indeed. So he left the place after a week and then it was downhill all the way.

*Were you angry with him for leaving it? I mean you had organized it.*

This is where the terrible, subtle trap comes into view. I'd read about it a thousand times, I'd talked about it with two people who'd been to Broadway Lodge. What happens is they take you over and you can only see it through their eyes. And you conspire with them to go on giving them sympathy. Well, what do you do to a friend? You give them sympathy. Peter lived with his mother and she gave him infinite quantities of sympathy. But the answer is that you shouldn't give them sympathy: you should throw them down the stairs. The experts say – and I believe them – that a drunk or drug addict will not kick the habit until they reach their bottom. That differs from person to person but until they get to the point where they know there's nothing left and they've stopped lying to themselves and they've faced what they're doing to themselves, then and then only can they start the climb up again. That's a simplified way, but it's the only way I can understand it and I've read about these things. And we didn't.

118

We gave him sympathy, we gave him whisky, and we shouldn't have done. We should have said, 'Get the hell off my door step, you filthy drunk.' But you can't say that to a man you've loved for thirty years.

*This 'we' being his little circle of friends?*

Yes, we all did it, we all did it and I remember one friend ringing me up – a mutual friend – and saying, 'Pete has just been here.' And he said, 'I'm feeling guilty. I should have said when he wanted a drink, "No".' And I said, 'Don't be silly, you couldn't say that. I couldn't say and didn't say it. You give him a drink.' But we should have done and I think, we all think: could we have saved him? That was the question and it'll go on ringing in my head. 'Could we have saved him?' I suppose the answer is yes, but only by those appallingly brutal methods.

*So the real act of friendship would have been to have been very, very cruel?*

That's exactly it and I couldn't, I simply couldn't bring myself to, because he had a fiery tongue, there's no question of that.

*Were you afraid of him?*

That's an interesting question: was I afraid of him? Well, he could be violent, though he never used violence to me or any of his close friends, I'm sure, but he had a violent streak in him there's no doubt about that. I don't think if I'd said, 'Go away, I'm not going to give you any more drink. I don't want to see you until you're sober,' he would have hit me. He would have just gone away and never spoken to me.

*When did he die?*

He must have died about five or six years ago.

*And what was your immediate response to the news?*

Well, it wasn't unexpected so it wasn't a shock in that sense, but my immediate thought, I think, was to picture him as so full of life, before it all happened. Because he was full of life, that is the only phrase. He was full of life, he was inquisitive, he had all sorts of talents. He was a quite exceptionally good cook and many is the wonderful meal I've eaten of his in France, where they lived. And what I saw, the image, the moment that I learned of his death, was him several years before: bright eyed and funny and fat – he grew very plump – but in a rather nice way so to speak. That was my first thought and then the second, of course, was that it had to happen. There was an autopsy which revealed that his liver was in such a condition that he couldn't have survived anyway, even if he'd gone off the drink then and there and never touched another drop. He would have died of it sooner or later.

*Did you ever talk with him about death?*

About death?

*Did you ever say, even jokingly, 'Look you're killing yourself, pull yourself together.'*

There again you see the conspiracy into which we are woven by such people with this terrible disease, and it is a hideous disease. We shied off – I did and most of his friends did – probably because of the conspiracy that we bound ourselves into and partly because we felt, I think rightly, that he wouldn't take any notice anyway. 'You're killing yourself,' you might say; and they all do these terrible subterfuges of saying, 'I haven't had a drink for three days now,' and so on. And then also he stopped writing, though he had a tape recorder and talked into it saying, 'I'm writing a book into a tape recorder, a lot of people do that.' But it wasn't, it was a sort of chatter. He left a book behind almost completed, but nobody would publish it, and again I come back to what I said a moment ago, and what we all say: 'Could we have saved him?' There was a point where we couldn't, but that was the condition of his liver. Could we have saved him? Maybe he was determined on this destructive course and there was nothing to be done about it.

*You had experienced other deaths, hadn't you?*

My mother, of course, and she had a marvellous ending. She was eighty-two and in perfect mental health and physical health, completely *compos mentis* to the end. She had a mild heart attack, went into hospital, was not in pain, was completely coherent, had another heart attack and died instantly – God send us all such an ending . . .

*How did Peter's death affect your life in the days after it? Were you conscious of a vacancy where he'd been?*

Yes very much so. He didn't want any funeral at all. He didn't want anything, any service, anything at all and he didn't want anybody there. The only person there was his mother. He was cremated and he said, 'I don't want any ceremony, religious or otherwise or memorial meeting or anything of that kind,' and his wishes were respected. Peter's father died much, much earlier than his mother, and when his father was cremated, Peter went up to Westmorland or somewhere like that, because his father was born there, to scatter his ashes on the hillside. That was the last sort of filial act for his father. I've always remembered that because Peter didn't have such an ending. After he died, first of all one had to think, 'Well it's a mercy in the end because he'd have got worse and worse and worse, and more agony for him.' Then as I implied a little earlier, the bad days were wiped out of one's memory and I always remember him now as the smiling, laughing, joking, cooking, talking friend that he was for so many years.

*Do you think it's important to prepare onself for death? It sounds to me as if he didn't really.*

No. I suppose there's something in all of us that tells us we're going to live forever. In our modern age – I've written about this a good deal, I think – there are people who really do seem to believe they are going to live forever and you have the absurd shenanigans people get up to with transplants, and God knows what. We're all going to die anyway. Only the other day I read about a devout Roman Catholic who was suffering from an apparently incurable disease and it was suggested that she should go to Lourdes to see if a miracle would happen. And she said, immensely sensibly, 'I'm not going to Lourdes, I'm going to die sooner or later anyway. If I go to Lourdes and this miracle happens, I'm not going to live for ever.' And I thought, 'Well good for you, dear, that's a very sensible argument.' We are going to die, we are finite, we're all going to die. It seems extraordinary; the fact is that from the day we are born the only thing we can be certain of, literally – whether we are going to be happy or rich or poor or put in prison or drink ourselves to death – we all know we're going to die, that's the only thing we know, the only thing we know for certain and yet we behave as though we're not. There is something good and grand, I believe, in that we think we're never going to die, but there's much more of absurdity in it.

*You said earlier that Peter's life was a disappointment and you threw off as an aside, 'Well my life's a disappointment, most people have to cope with disappointment.' Knowing that, can you contemplate a situation where perhaps you would actually want to destroy yourself as he did?*

I can. There could only be one form. It would be that I am suffering from an incurable disease or condition and it was giving me great pain on the one hand and I was becoming incoherent in my mind on the other. Then, and since I'm going to die shortly in this postulated situation, then I think I could take an overdose of sleeping pills or whatever it might be. But that's the only circumstance. Because the life force in us all is tremendous. It is, actually. Look at those skeletons that came out of Belsen at the end of the war, but alive, although God knows millions were murdered. There they were: skeletons, literally skeletons; but something in them kept them going, and of course we know people have been tortured and imprisoned unjustly and lived in hell and that life spark would not go out for them. I admire that greatly. I think that up to a point I could do that, in prison for instance, but ultimately I don't think I would in those circumstances that I mentioned. I think I would rather turn it off.

*Were there any lessons for you in Peter's death?*

One damn good lesson is not to become a drunkard, but that's one danger I've never been in and never will be in. I couldn't become a drunk or a drug addict, thank heaven. I have other vices. That was the only lesson and that was so obvious it was hardly worth discussing. I don't think otherwise . . .

*What about not giving in to despair?*

I hadn't really thought of it in those terms but that's a contrast with Peter. I never give in; perhaps it's an illusion but I still tell myself, 'No, no it's not so bad,' etcetera and that's what I do do. Even if it *is* so bad I say, 'No, no it's not so bad.' That's also a kind of cover up but I think a rather better one – at least a rather more useful one at any rate – to say this awful thing has happened but you'll forget about it. Incidentally it's usually true, not always, but it's usually true; *tout casse, tout passe, tout lasse*: everything sorts itself out.

*You said you have no conventional religious faith; do you see death then as not a doorway but a tragedy?*

No, I don't think of it as a tragedy and I think it couldn't possibly be a tragedy because we all have to go through it. I mean if someone is knocked down by a motor car and killed that is a tragedy, but death itself is no tragedy as far as I'm concerned. I have no conventional faith, that is to say I do not adhere to any church, but I don't believe that death is the end. That I'm firmly convinced of. What follows it I don't know, but I can't persuade myself that we are here and it's all meaningless and we die and are buried. I think there is, I'm convinced there is, more to it than that. There's something survives death, you can call it spirit, soul, I don't mind; but I believe something survives. What happens to it I'm not sure. The most attractive form I think is the Buddhist philosophy where you go round and round and round on the wheel, learning and learning and learning each time until you finally get off the wheel into nirvana and I rather think that whether the Buddhists have got it right or not something like that is there: that we have to learn through lives – not life – *lives*, with reincarnation. I don't know, I've never really worked it out on squared paper and decided exactly, but I do believe that there is something after death which you have to experience and go on experiencing. I think something like that is probably true. I shall die thinking it certainly though I may have a nasty shock afterwards.

*Do you think that the lives of the dead – your mother, your friend – become a part of you?*

In a sense, yes I do. I think two things. First of all, one's close relatives on the one hand and one's friends on the other do become part of you, and I think their deaths, in another category, also do. For instance, one thinks of Peter's death as a tragedy. It was. He wasted his life by drinking himself to death; he had many years before him. I think death – a good death or a bad death – is woven into our lives in some way from somebody close. I think because they affected, genuinely affected, moved, stirred, did something to your life, you incorporate something of that in their death.

# === 8 ===

# CHRIS PATTEN

*The Rt. Hon. Chris Patten, former Chairman of the*
*Conservative Party and now Governor of Hong Kong,*
*recalls his mother Joan.*

The thing I remember most clearly about my mother is that she
was extremely pretty. I can remember even as a little boy being
very proud of the fact that she was the prettiest mum in the
playground. She was – I think she'd have used the word
'bandbox'. She was always very concerned about her appearance.
She had pretty brown curly hair, great wide forehead, beautiful
blue eyes; a handsome woman and curvaceous in a rather
Victorian way. Much of her later years was spent going on diets to
try to stop becoming too curvaceous. She wasn't remotely
intellectual. She was very tactile, very practical and enormously
loving and I think loved her children (and perhaps, I mean no
disrespect to my sister, but perhaps me especially) inordinately.
So we grew up cocooned with affection and love.

*So you were very close to her.*

Yes. Yes, and I think you don't realize how much other people
pour into you until it's too late really to do anything about it, so
I think I was much closer to her than I realized at the time.

*When you went away to university and then started your career in*
*politics, did your relationship change or were you still close to her?*

I was still close to her but I think one goes through – perhaps it's an inevitable part of growing up and becoming independent – I think one tends to go through a rather selfish phase. And I think one can also (if one's not careful) become a bit grand and I think I did. I think it affected my relationship with my father more than my relationship with my mother; and I certainly had the opportunity, because my mother lived for longer than my father, of re-establishing a sensible relationship with her. I always regret the fact that my father didn't live longer and that I wasn't able to get past that rather silly phase of being a clever young man, and grow up in order to establish a proper adult relationship with him.

*Did your mother ever show you that she was hurt by that?*

Not really, I don't think, because she wouldn't have wanted her emotions to be seen as part of the relationship in a funny way, except in so far as they were positive. She occasionally indicated that she would have liked me to have spent a bit more time at home or have 'phoned up more often or have written home – in the way that parents do – but no more than that, no. I think that she was very proud of what I was doing – slightly surprised – but extremely proud of it and that therefore made up for any personal inadequacies in the way I treated her.

*Why do you say she was slightly surprised?*

I don't think she would have reckoned on me going into politics or public life, or maybe she would, but I'd never shown any great interest in politics as a kid. I was interested in acting and writing and sport and went through a phase which must have been very distracting for her though she was a convert to Catholicism – I don't think, with respect, that it was ever a major part of her life – I went through a phase when I covered the dining-room table with wine glasses and candles and spent a lot of time pretending to be a priest or indeed the Pope. So I'd had a go at most other careers but never really at politics.

*Can you describe for me the night your mother died?*

Yes, it is an extraordinary, improbable story which will involve a certain amount of name-dropping but let me plunge in. At the time, I'd been in the House of Commons about six months, and I'd just become the Parliamentary Private Secretary to Norman St John Stevas who was the leader of the House of Commons. Parliamentary Private Secretary isn't a minister, you're a sort of parliamentary dogsbody and when your minister is speaking from the front bench you sit behind ready to dart off and get bits of paper from civil servants for him or her or do whatever other services may be required from time to time. It was delightful doing the job for Norman.

He was answering a debate in the House of Commons which was supposed to finish at seven o'clock but was plainly going to go on much later and it caused very considerable problems because he was due to go off and do *Question Time* – it was I think the first or second season of the *Question Time* television pro-gramme with Robin Day – and he turned to me on the front bench and said, 'You must go off and telephone the BBC because I'm not going to be able to make that broadcast. I simply don't think the debate will finish in time.'

So realizing this was a rather disagreeable job I had to perform I went off and 'phoned up the BBC producer who said, 'But this is impossible, he must come on.' So I said, 'He can't, he's answering a debate in the House of Commons.' She said, 'Well there'll have to be somebody else, who else can do it?' And I said, 'I don't know, I'll go and ask him.' I went back and spoke to him and he said, 'Well, you must do it.' Rather embarrassed, I told the BBC producer that they were going to get me, which she obviously didn't think was a tremendous catch. The others on the programme were real stars: there was John Rae, then the Headmaster of Westminster, and there was Neil Kinnock who was then I think the Labour Party Shadow Education spokesman.

Anyway I had a moment before I went off to the television studio and thought I must 'phone up my mother, my mum, and tell her that her son was about to appear on this glamorous television programme. So I 'phoned her up and told her I was going to be on the programme. Spoke to her very briefly.

I then went off and did the programme. Everybody was very nice to me – Neil Kinnock especially nice – and didn't knock me all about the place because I was unbriefed and very young and wet behind the ears. I did the programme, went home bathed in triumph, and my mother died that night. So it was the last time that I spoke to her, an extraordinary coincidence, and one must hope that she died reasonably happy having seen me on the box.

*She was probably very proud.*

I hope so. She had been very proud of both my sister and me. I said earlier that I think she invested a great deal of herself in us. She pushed us, not inordinately hard, but she was always very keen that we worked hard at school and working hard at school was part of her vision of life. You had clean shoes and washed your ears and brushed your teeth and worked at primary school, knew your catechism and did well in class. And she'd been consistently proud as I went through primary school and came top of the class and got a scholarship to an independent school, a sort of direct grant school. And then she'd been proud as I'd ploughed through and got university scholarships and all that. So it was nice for her that it finished like that. I think other people's enjoyment of one's own laurels is much the nicest part of earning them.

*Did you think afterwards that you wouldn't have 'phoned her if it hadn't been for this accident?*

Absolutely, I certainly wouldn't have 'phoned her had it not been for that. And the next morning when my stepfather 'phoned with this astonishing news and I went round to see her body I can remember being very confused by the contingent factor in history, by the accidental nature of having spoken to her for the last time.

*How old was she?*

She was sixty. She'd just had a check-up and had been pro-nounced pretty fit and then she went to sleep that night and didn't wake up. So my stepfather had woken with the cold body beside him. And I can remember going in to see her. I've seen both my parents and my stepfather dead just as I've seen my children born which gives me an extraordinarily strong feeling about the sanctity of life. I remember being in a way surprised by how fine she looked, because certainly as she'd got older the fact that she wore a great deal of make-up had sometimes meant that in the morning she didn't look as spectacular as she did the night before. I'm always rather pleased that my wife uses hardly any make-up so I always recognize the person I wake up with! But I was surprised in the light of that, that when I saw my mother and kissed her she looked wonderfully fine, as though chiselled out of marble, but cold.

*In the days that followed, how did her death actually affect you?*

I've always been very guilty about being able to cope with death more easily than I think should be the case. Largely by trying to let the waters close as quickly as possible and largely by trying to forget. I don't think that could always be possible. I don't think it could conceivably be possible for a young child losing a parent or for a parent losing a young child. I think it's probably easier as an older adult losing a friend or particularly if the friend is rather older. Or losing, as an adult, a parent. But I felt guilty at forgetting so quickly – deliberately making myself try to forget and get on with things.

*I'm curious that you use the word 'forget'. You say that you tried to forget and get on with things. Surely you don't actually mean 'forget'?*

Yes I do, I mean literally try to stop thinking of someone and it therefore becomes – which is what makes it such an inadequate human response – it therefore becomes more difficult with the passage of time to remember them again. Trying to recall my parents demands more concentration now than it should and I have to think hard to anecdotalize or to remember and to get a grip on particular personal feelings about them. So it's a bad way of trying to cope with bereavement, I think, but perhaps we all have to come at bereavement in our own distinctive fashion.

*Do you think that it's a rather male way of coping: running away from feelings?*

I think not necessarily. You may be right, but I heard a wonderful story the other day from a friend about somebody he'd been working with professionally, a woman who had no children and she and her husband had been virtually the only adults in their respective lives for years. Her husband ran a small business rather successfully, they did everything together, all their hobbies together. One day he dropped dead and all she could do was to go into the office and take over the company. She doubled the turnover, she did wonderfully at it, the one thing she couldn't bring herself to do was wind up his clocks, and then one day five or six years later she found that she could go round the house and wind up all the clocks again and then she could remember him once again.

*Is there any parallel to that in your own life? Was it after that initial period where you worked and attempted to forget, not think about her, was there a period later on which perhaps mirrored that period in your younger life where you as it were came closer to her memory?*

I think that I always find it easier to talk about somebody who has died, or revisit a place or an institution which I've much loved, after some time. I found it, for example, impossible to go back to Oxford for years after I'd left it; so maybe for me it's easier to remember at a safe distance.

*Just over ten years on.*

Yes, exactly.

*When a parent dies, is there any sense in the child within you, of moving upwards, moving into their place in the hierarchy?*

Very much so. I mentioned earlier that I've seen all my – I say all because I've had a stepfather as well – my parents and my stepfather all dead, and buried them all and spoken at all their funerals with some difficulty. Seen them into the ground. And I've also had the enormous privilege of seeing all my children born – always from, as it were, the safe end of the operation – and I think that experience does give you an enormous sense of moving on and gives a sort of context to the feelings of *déjà vu* one has very frequently as a parent. I think one has to learn from your experience of being a child in order to be a half-adequate parent and invariably one finds oneself doing as a parent precisely those things that as a child one resented about one's own parents.

*Do you ever find yourself saying things to your children that your mother said to you?*

Oh yes. I think though that a particular problem for a parent is while providing your children with the love and comfort and warmth and nest that all children deserve, to encourage them to be independent as well. In a way the fact that I was so happy and comfortable and loved when I was growing up played on a rather unadventurous side of my character and I think that I was therefore less resourceful and less independent minded when I was in my late teens and early twenties than I should have been. I don't mean by that that I should have been selfish, because I was pointing out earlier that I think I was much too selfish and didn't show enough regard for my parents at that stage. But I should have done more things with my life and I want to ensure that my own children – while they always have somewhere to come back to – feel as though they've got the strength and the resource in their own characters to go off and do their own things.

*Push them out of the nest?*

Yes, it's a terribly difficult thing for a parent to do. My wife and I were contemplating the prospect only the other day when we suddenly found ourselves on our own for a weekend at home with all the children flown in different directions and it was awfully difficult getting used to the silence.

*You are a practising Christian – a Roman Catholic – were there ever times after the death of either of your parents when your faith was tested?*

No. I don't find it remotely easy to comprehend what C.S. Lewis called the problem of pain. I cannot construct an adequate rational argument to, for instance, explain to a parent why they should have borne a handicapped child as part of God's destiny or why they should lose a child. I can't find an adequate explanation or apologetics for mass starvation in the Horn of Africa. I can't find explanations for those things. C.S. Lewis is, I guess, about as near as I've come to being persuaded and that's something else I've just tried to shut out. So it's been for me a question of belief and another reflection of Pascal's wager: you just have to hope you're right.

*So your mother died at sixty hoping for her retirement – very young – so in a sense she was cheated of what she wanted. Did you never have that inner voice which cried out, 'Well it's not fair'?*

Not so much as, for example, my wife must inevitably have done.

She was in the position of never knowing her father because he died while she was in the womb and then she lost her mother when she was sixteen. Now there I can imagine beating one's fists on the door in rage. But I didn't feel that about my parents. To be honest what I felt about losing both my parents at that sort of age – my father at fifty-eight, my mother at sixty and none of my grandparents lived to a very great age – was that maybe there is a lesson in genetics . . .

*Do you think much about your own death?*

Not enough. I think one should be able – particularly as a Christian believing in an after-life – I think one should try to ensure that one has the time to prepare for one's death and that one learns not to fear death. It may be more difficult for Christians of my sort of age, because at an impressionable time one was brought up in the great hell-fire tradition before Vatican II and all that. So it may be that we have stamped on us indelibly some fears of what comes after, which we have to learn to cope with. But maybe fear of the unknown is the same for anybody, whatever those early experiences and whatever their early teaching.

*Seeing your parents die at relatively young ages – does that make you want to cram the time? Does it make you feel urgent?*

It does a bit. I think that one of the great crimes in life is to be bored and to lay about; one should attempt to fill every minute and every hour and every day. It doesn't mean reckless activity, but it does mean actually using your time. I always say when I visit schools and I'm obliged to address some poor unsuspecting class of fifteen or sixteen year olds, that being bored is an awful self-indulgence and an awful crime.

*Do you have a strong sense of her presence?*

I do as I talk and the more I talk and think about her the more I'm able to conjure pictures of her out of the air and to remember some of the romance of her and my father's life. They did – in a 1930s, 1940s, very middle-class way – have rather a romantic life: meeting when my father was playing in a band at a dance and enduring the disapproval of both sets of parents because my father was not only a drummer in a band but also a *Catholic* drummer in a band, which was even more difficult, I suspect, for my mother's parents to understand.

*When I asked if you had a strong sense of her presence I was actually thinking of it not so much as we speak, but returning to faith. Because it seems to me that if you believe in a life after death, which I don't, that you must believe that that person is somehow watching you, watching over you. Is that true?*

Yes, to some extent. I began as a child as a Christian praying to the Saints and All Souls with a sense of all my relations sitting up there waiting for those of us on earth to arrive some time. I can't think of the after-life like that now. I don't find that image a helpful or likely one: that one somehow is waiting to arrive at a celestial St George's Hill, Weybridge, and there will be the massed Pattens from past generations. I find that a difficult concept. I don't know what I think the after-life will be like but I just hope that I am able to learn not to fear it. I think not fearing death is the greatest triumph.

*Looking back at the night that she died ten years later, what are your feelings about it?*

My feelings are. . . There are two very strong feelings I have about my mother. The first is that I hope that she didn't endure pain. The second relates to a rather arcane subject, certainly for all those who haven't had at any stage in their lives to learn the Six Sins against the Holy Ghost – at least I think it was six. As I recall from my catechism, I can recall despair being one of them.

And the sixth was final impenitence. And I just hope that she died happy with what she was, with her relationships and what she was trying to do, and didn't die feeling cross about anything or cross with anybody. Final impenitence. I can't remember which novel it comes in, it may be a William Trevor novel, in which somebody has described it in terms of the old man dying and shouting, 'Get that great bird out of the room': a terrible description of the Holy Ghost. But to die feeling generous and not frightened and not in pain . . .

*And at peace.*

In so far as you ever can, yes.

*Is guilt a part of the package that you carry now?*

I think that I have a fairly well-developed sense of guilt and need to lay off that for a bit; but yes I feel guilty that I wasn't a better son and I hope I don't ever feel guilty that I haven't been a better parent. But I expect I will.

# 9

# BARRIE RUTTER

*The actor Barrie Rutter has played leading roles in many
productions at the National Theatre and on television. His baby son Harry
died in his cot.*

Harry was born on the first of July 1984. We'd received the news
only two weeks before that he was breech, so a day was booked for
a Caesarean and he came about ten days before that. He decided
to come and I had no petrol in the car. We got to the hospital in
Leamington Spa on a tablespoonful of juice. I was desperately
hoping the flipping thing would get there, whisked in about nine
o'clock in the morning, Sunday morning. Carol said what was
happening, and it was straight up to delivery, and she was
absolutely magnificent because if she hadn't been wonderful
they'd have knocked her out and they would have done a
Caesarean. Her own guts and everything kept her awake and she
delivered the baby breech, and it was all over by half past
twelve.

*You saw him born?*

Oh yes, I was there, yes.

*Did you very much want a son?*

I suppose that old macho thing of 'I hope it's a lad this time' can't
help but cross your mind; the mind's a very quick thing, you

can't help but think like that at times. But quite frankly I wasn't too bothered about it and I thought it would be a girl anyway.

*Did you have other children?*

Briony was coming up to two when he was born, she was a year and nine months.

*What was he like?*

He was tough, he was a really tough little baby and his eyes hadn't decided what colour they were going to be by the time he died, they were changing. He was really tough . . . I think my wife could probably tell you better.

*Do you have a very vivid mental picture of him?*

Visually his face – no I don't. You know that relaxation you get when the second child is always easier and there's the first child to deal with anyway so there's less fuss, there's less pictures taken? We have no pictures of Harry except for his christening. We didn't take pictures in his stages. We have one with Carol holding him with Briony in the bath and some other kids in the bath as well, all having a bath together, and that's about the only picture we have in the fourteen weeks since he was christened.

*Tell me about the day he died.*

I was on stage and I'd been shopping. I was in *Animal Farm* at the National Theatre. I'd been shopping in Covent Garden and I'll tell you what I bought. I walked round those stalls in Covent Garden and there were some little cockerel brooches, stick-ons, and I bought Briony a two-tone white and yellow one, and I bought Harry a black one. That was at twelve pm and he died just after two o'clock or between two and three o'clock.

The matinée started at two o'clock in the afternoon. By the

time the stage management had got the news we were well into the second half, so they had to wait until the end of the show because I never left the stage in *Animal Farm*. So the Stage Manager came into the dressing room at the end and said, 'I've got some very bad news to tell you.' She was smoking in my dressing room as well, so I knew it was something bad because I'm a bit of an old woman about smoking: I don't allow anyone to smoke in the dressing room. And Harry was the last one in the world that I thought. I thought it may have been Carol or maybe – again when the mind works really quickly in the millionth of a second you say, 'Who can it be?' – I thought at first it might be my in-laws, that Carol had received news from America. Then I immediately thought of my father and then either Carol or Briony, and when she said, 'Harry – your son,' I was shocked at the choice that the Gods had made. Because his name hadn't run through my disaster computer, if you like.

*Can you remember what you said?*

I think I said, 'Oh that poor woman.'

*Meaning?*

Meaning Carol.

*You thought of her pain first?*

I don't know whether I did think of her pain, I thought of her. I simply said, 'Oh that poor woman.' And at that point again I was stood there in half costume, I'd only just washed me white make-up off me face, with all the accoutrements of the theatre around me. I know at that point I was thinking, 'How the hell am I going to get through the evening show?' And, 'I hope everybody stays with her until I get home.' And then I 'phoned home and it became . . . it just became obvious that I was going to get my clothes on and get straight in the car. I just went. And I drove very fast and I was sort of hoping for a police car to stop me and I had the radio – it was the football results – on just full volume: Arsenal versus whatever, it didn't matter, it was just full volume. I kept it on Radio 4 so that it was constant talking all the time and driving as fast as the car would go. I think I was hoping for a police car to stop me so that they could drive me or offer to drive me, I don't know. And I got home and I opened the door and Carol rushed into my arms and said, 'I'm sorry, I'm sorry, I'm sorry,' and I said, 'No blame, no blame, don't blame yourself.' A couple of days later she said again in a very sort of marked way to me, 'I'm sorry, I'm sorry, I'm sorry,' and I said, 'Look there's no blame, because', I said, 'if you blame yourself I'll blame you, because', I said, 'I'll be entitled to, so there's no blame.' And then of course all the women that were in our house who had been sitting with Carol they all sort of got up and put their coats on. I appealed to at least one or two of them to stay; I wasn't a knight on a white charger coming in to the rescue and therefore everything was alright, I needed massaging as well and I needed help. So one or two of them got the message and stayed for me as well.

*Did you try to find out immediately what exactly had happened? What was the sequence of events that led up to his death in his cot?*

I didn't try to find out immediately. I didn't find out for a matter of hours I think, if not the next day. He was asleep and she'd been out shopping with a friend and they let him sleep. And she was in the kitchen making his lunch and this is what amazed the coroner's policeman when he came round, because he was asking things like, 'Had you just fed him?' because it was at lunchtime. And Carol said, 'No, he didn't have a morsel of food in him, he was sleeping. I was letting him sleep, we'd been out shopping and he'd been roughed about in the crib and I let him sleep.' When the coroner did the autopsy of course he said, 'I don't need to see these people, there was nothing wrong with this child.' Unexplained death.

*When you use the word 'blame', do you think now that your wife was actually asking you for forgiveness? That she did feel guilty because she was there?*

Yes, I know. . . I don't know. . . It's a bit silly to speculate really, but I was convinced that if she blamed herself then I would blame her as well and I think along that path would lie the destruction of our marriage.

*How did other people cope with you? You say that friends had obviously come round to be with your wife, then you arrived and some of them went, and you needed massage. Did you get that sort of help from close friends?*

From some.

*Did you feel they understood what you were going through?*

No, and I didn't want them to neither.

*Why?*

Well, taken to its ultimate they'd have to go through the death of a child, that's what I mean. I mean often people would say, 'I know how you feel,' and I'd round on them very angrily and say, 'You fucking don't know and I don't want you to know neither.' We had a counselling lady come round and that proved a real non-event. I don't know what we expected from it but it was as if she could offer some light or some reason or some insight but she couldn't. And again, we were doing things with each other and through friends that was far better in helping us than a counselling lady.

*What sort of things?*

I don't know, but we got on with it. That sounds crass doesn't it:

'we got on with it'. The very next morning, Sunday morning, we stripped all his things out; for instance, we returned his pram. He had a wonderful old fashioned fifties – if not earlier – pram that we'd borrowed off a friend up the road and we wheeled that back and I remember we passed a father and son in the field. They were working on their tractors but they couldn't stop and they didn't stop. Carol thought that really rather remarkable, because his wife had been in our house on the afternoon previously with her, but the men couldn't stop. And it is a very small community we live in, a very tiny road that we walked to deliver back this pram. But no, they just tractored on and just sort of nodded their heads.

*Did you talk to other men about what you were suffering? I'm saying men in particular because often in a case like this all the sympathy is directed at the wife, not at the husband, and after all it was your baby too.*

Yes I did. Again I can't really remember individual discussions other than with the poet Tony Harrison, my friend and mentor, and he said, 'In time you will learn to celebrate, really celebrate the ninety-eight days that he lived.' Again what he was hinting at (or at least what I took) was that if you don't, then it's despair and that is a very black road.

*Is it very hard to accept something as random as that though? That it was nobody's fault?*

It was for me because it was totally random and I knew I was really angry and I knew I was looking for a fight somewhere and I was really bitterly angry at it. It came to it one day. It was a year to his birth, and I was in *The Mysteries* at the Lyceum Theatre, from the National Theatre, and one actor was always perpetually drunk. And it was the day after, it was the second of July, and I was playing Herod, the killer of all the boy children. I mean, it was easier to play it and say the words than it was when I watched it. But this actor came off drunk, ranting and raving about 'If you want to redirect this play, Rutter' and I really was an inch off knocking seven bells of shit out of him. I might have lost the fight but I think I'd have won it because I was desperate for a real physical manifestation of my rage against the Gods, against the randomness of it. I think someone else stepped in and it got controlled and I've never felt that anger since. I've certainly not felt it since the birth of Rowan Jessie, our second daughter, because we were going to stop at two children, so whatever my grief is now, it is always bittersweet because there she is, three and a half, blonde and rather wonderful and her big sister thinks she's terrific. There was three of us having a baby when Carol was pregnant with Rowan and she was very careful to bring Briony in so it was Briony's baby as well.

*How did Briony cope with her little brother's death?*

We of course had her in our bed, you can imagine. We heard every bloody breath she took and any little rustle. I mean I sat up just like Dracula from sleep and so did Carol. Now obviously that couldn't go on, but just for that period. We only lost our temper with her once and that was the morning of the funeral which she didn't go to. We were having our bath and putting clothes on to go to church and she spotted the atmosphere then and that was the only time – I don't know whether it was me or Carol, I think it was Carol – lost her rag with her, out of sheer grief of her own.

*What happened at the funeral?*

Well, the first thing I saw when I walked in the church . . . his godmother Mary had bought him a car and that couldn't go in the coffin with him, though lots of things did go in the coffin with him, but they'd put this beautiful wooden car on the foot of the coffin. That was the first thing visually, the second thing was how bloody little this coffin was. But Carol had also bought him ninety-eight daffodil bulbs, one for each day, and trying to see these men from the undertakers trying to fit ninety-eight daffodil bulbs on such a short and small little plot of ground was very funny and they kept looking up at me as if to say, 'We can't do it, Barrie.' They're trying to work this jigsaw out, because it was a very tiny plot.

*And did they manage?*

They just managed. So in the spring it's a blaze of daffodils.

*What does it say on the tombstone?*

Ah well, now the tombstone. We decided to have a piece of Portland Stone for the stone and we were going to go down to Portland to the quarry and pick up a stone. Now we may have been a little naïve but that's what we thought we were going to do. Outside the National Theatre you'll see a stone circle geometrically carved in odd shapes, but a circle, and that was cut by one of the top stonemasons in Britain, at that point, in 1985. And he bought all the Portland Stone off the old Kensington Town Hall and he was outside the National for years and he used to come in the canteen and have tea and that. And I didn't know it was him, I didn't know he was the artist but I said to him one day, 'Is all that Portland Stone out there?'
And he said, 'Yes, why?'
And I said, 'Well is anything for sale?'
Obviously he was very guarded. He looked at me and said, 'Why?'
Anyway I told him and he said, 'Come on, pick your stone, I'll carve it for you.'
It's amazing how large a piece of stone you have to have because Harry's stone is a nice little chunky thing with a smooth face, and about a third of it is under the ground. And he carved it for me and put the smooth face on and he told me already he didn't want

anything for it, so I bought him a couple of bottles of champagne
and he didn't even want them, he just wouldn't take them. So I
took the stone home and then another friend Max is a trained
artist and he said, 'I'll engrave it for you, would you let me do
that?' And then I asked Tony Harrison if I could put on one of his
little quotes that he wrote in a television piece called *The Big H*.
It just simply says, 'Every Babe's worth Gold, Frankincense and
Myrrh'. And that also is on Harry's sampler which Carol's sister
Roberta in Texas made, and Carol put it up on the Friday night
on the wall; it arrived from Texas all done and 'Every Babe's
Worth Gold, Frankincense and Myrrh' in celebration and little
pictures of us in the needlepoint and they put it up together; he
was there in the crib and she put it up on the wall on the Saturday
morning; it was Saturday afternoon he died.

And a year later, we put the stone in – a year to the day after
he'd been buried – and there was quite a few of us went down
there. We took a gallon of wine, and cement to cement the stone
in and there are secret little pockets in the stone below ground
where little treasures and things went in – I don't mean gold and
silver – but I mean treasures from us to him, and letters, and we
cemented it in and sat round and had a party. There was at least
half a dozen kids.

*Do you think rituals like that are important?*

I do. Fire was another one. The day of the funeral we went in the
field – we have a little bit of meadow-land right opposite our
house – and it was a beautiful day in October and we went into
the field and had a big fire, just sat round, and we were the last
round it, just me and Carol with a bottle of whisky.

*You mentioned that Tony Harrison, whose words are on the tombstone,
said that you would have to learn to celebrate, and yet you said that a
year afterwards you nearly got into a fight with somebody because you
felt such rage. Has it been at all possible for you to reach a condition of
celebration, as he advised?*

Absolutely, but it's not . . . the water is not absolutely clear, is it? Rowan's birth, her christening and her life ever since and also what we've done as a foursome as well . . . I mean, this is really to put a heavy mantle on Rowan and I don't mean to because we've all done it together, Briony our eldest as well. I think it's just that the tears are a different colour now. I mean it's not all of loss, because we now have a daughter we wouldn't have had because we were going to stop at two. But I miss him.

*You've talked very movingly about how Rowan, your second daughter, has been a great gift to you, but after Harry died, did you have that experience of not feeling you wanted another child? People often say when a baby dies, 'You can have another baby,' as if you could replace a child. Did you reject that thought?*

I never did, mainly because Carol was so positive that we would. We had bloody great difficulty getting pregnant again, that was probably our own mental anguish over a period of about eighteen months, two years, but no, I knew, I knew I wanted another child. But I did wait for Carol to say. I don't think I initiated the idea of another; hell, who knows whether I started it first or she started it. What does it matter? She did say, I know, 'I'd like my body to have another child.' And so we did and Rowan is now three and a half, and a renegade! Do you know what Rowan means? We couldn't escape symbolism obviously, and Rowan in its medieval meaning of the word means 'second harvest' or literally 'aftermath'.

*Were you glad that you had a girl?*

Oh I wasn't bothered, I mean my joy was a child, I really wasn't bothered. I cried like mad out of joy when Briony was born, and I cried like mad when Harry was born. That was coupled with the anguish I'd seen Carol go through with a breech birth and it was just a real flood of relief. And when Rowan was born I think my tears hit the back wall, just a real spurt of tearful joy.

*We've called this series* A Perspective for Living. *I wonder is it possible that the totally unexpected death of a baby boy at fourteen weeks can give that?*

Yes, apart from another child being positive. Just on a little personal note, whenever anyone from now on close to me has a death around them, I just hope I will never say 'I know how you feel.'

*Because you feel that grief is always absolutely particular, unique?*

It always is, yes, it's always unique. But my big sort of wide-armed embrace for them, would be to tell them to grieve, not to stop it. In that I was told I was very unmale or not stereotypically male; I let it all go, I let it all go, I didn't stop grieving until I chose to. I never refused anything, I didn't actually go on a binge of drink and food but I never actually refused anything. It's only a recent thing that I've recollected but it's amazing how many times we say 'No thank you' to a very everyday normal thing; whether it's at leisure, or at work or at play we say 'No, thank you,' and I never for about eighteen months refused a thing that was food and drink.

*Did people come round with things like that? Was that one way of people coping with your grief, to give you things?*

Yes they did, they did.

*That anger which anybody would think would be the first thing that you would feel, a terrible rage that this baby should be taken, is it still with you now? I mean, when you go to his grave do you feel anger, or is there acceptance?*

No I don't feel . . . oh, I think I would be foolish to say I don't feel any anger, but it's not as much, it's not as much. And we always try to make his grave a pleasant place to visit, we talk

149

about tickling Harry's tummy and things like that when we wash the stone down. And we have a good neighbour down the road who has geese and every Easter there's three big goose eggs for our children. There's always one for Harry and we take it down, we put it on top of the stone and the girls will help it to stop rolling off with a chocolate Easter egg or two, and we know the fox is going to come, but we say, 'Well that will be good because Harry will like that, the fox getting the free food.' And it's all in the girls' lives, it's all their dialogue, it's all joyous. I have my quiet moments with him, but as a family the visits to the grave are always a joy.

*And there's always five of you?*

There's always five of us – yes.

# ═══10═══

# CLARE SHORT

*Clare Short is the Labour Member of Parliament for
Ladywood, Birmingham. Her father, Frank, was
a teacher.*

*What sort of man was your father?*

He was a very fine man. I went last week to a cancer hospice and
one of the nurses there was at the school where he taught, and she
was saying what a lovely man he was. He was tall and thin. He
was a teacher in an inner-city school and really cared about
children and their learning. He was from Ireland, from Crossmaglen, which is just three miles north of the border, and deeply
resented the fact that his country had been partitioned – a real
Irish nationalist. He was a natural intellectual, he just liked ideas
and talking about them, and we grew up in that kind of house
where there was good conversation, often political, around the
table. He was very undomineering and yet powerfully influential;
people looked to him and listened to what he said and almost
everyone who knew him really sort of admired and liked him. He
wasn't a very warm, noisy person; he was kind of quietish and
understated if anything, but very fine.

*You had four sisters and two brothers. Did he differentiate between the
boys or the girls or was he an early feminist?*

His great, deep, hidden secret is he was a member of the National

Association of Schoolmasters at the time when it opposed equal pay for women teachers . . . outrageous! But the way we were brought up, we were all just expected to share the washing-up and doing the beds but what we achieved at school was of equal importance. There was no differentiation between the boys and the girls. It's just he always liked the littlest one; but we all had our turn at being it. We were all close to him really.

*How did your mother fit in with all this? Was she an equal influence?*

My mum was the big, warm, loving, always-there-for-us, classical mother, but she sacrificed a lot of her intellectual life and so on, to the bringing up of the children. She must have been an enormously bright little girl. My grandad worked at Lucas's; she passed the scholarship to the girls' Catholic Grammar School that I went to in Birmingham, but in those days there were few scholarships and she was pulled out of school when my granny had her youngest child and there were difficulties with the pregnancy. She married my dad when she was twenty-two and there were seven of us and then in her forties she went back to work in Lucas's and joined the Labour Party and became active and became a person in her own right.

*How was your father's influence on you different from that of your mother?*

My father's was political, intellectual; my mum's was the absolute security of being loved which is very important when you're a child; and I think it affects your adulthood when you've had that kind of security. It's silly in a way to attribute completely different things to them, but that's the kind of combination: the warmth and lovingness my mum gave us which we learned to do to other people; and the ideas and the generosity of ideas and a kind of confidence about ideas and standing up for what you knew to be true, whatever the world said and however unpopular it was, from Dad. For example I was ten at the time of the Suez crisis and all the kids in my school were singing, 'We'll throw Nasser in the Suez Canal,' and I got them together and explained that they were wrong and that the Egyptians were entitled to their own canal. But also there were pictures on the wall at home of the Soviet invasion of Hungary and we knew that was wrong too. There weren't any lectures, that's just the way it was. We just grew up knowing that what was right was right and what was wrong was wrong and it doesn't matter what the world says; if they shout at you you've just got to stand up for it.

*When you became a teenager – and you're a very strong personality – did you have any clashes with your dad?*

I certainly had clashes with my mum and got locked out and had to climb in and that stuff. With my dad, no, I don't think so particularly. Certainly there was a period when I wasn't so close to him and then I was closer to him again when I was a bit older.

*So what made you close again?*

Just life and respect and love and he was just a lovely man and I really honoured him; and so we used to talk and when I became an MP he was still alive and living in Birmingham in the constituency – that's where I grew up – and he was getting old then and I used to go home at the end of the day, and he was there, and he loved to hear my stories of what I'd been up to and we'd sit and he'd sip whisky and I'd regale him.

*Was he proud of you?*

Yes, I think he was.

*Was there any sense do you think in which by becoming an MP you fulfilled ambitions he might have had?*

He was intensely political but we never thought about any of us standing for office. There was never any kind of self-seeking in it. So I don't think he would have ever thought of himself being a politician. The things he did politically he did just for the causes 'cos he believed in them; so it was a bit of a surprise that I ended up there. He wasn't a proud man but I know secretly – not secretly even, just quietly – he liked it.

*How did he approach old age and illness?*

He had terrible bronchitis – great difficulty in breathing. His intellect was in no way diminished, so he remained himself completely, but his body wore out and it became a real sort of struggle for him just to be able to breathe and get up and eat. I think it made him tired, struggling with his body.

*Did he get depressed?*

Not depressed – a bit exasperated sometimes and I can remember him saying that he'd been thinking about his childhood a lot when he'd been ill, and it wasn't that long before he died. It was as though he knew it was coming: his body was just wearing out and it was becoming too much like hard work to carry on being alive.

*Before it got to that stage did you ever imagine his death?*

If I did, not really realistically. I mean we all knew he was ill and everybody was around and wanted to be close to him and that's sort of treasuring because you know you won't have somebody forever, but I don't think you can imagine it. Like my mother, she's seventy odd – she'll live for ages 'cos my granny lived to be ninety odd – but I think, 'Well one day my mother will die.' I *think* that, but it's not the same as it happening. Anyway, I was at the House of Commons; I was reading on the Wages Bill. Then I got this message: 'Urgent – ring the switchboard,' so I popped out, and they said, 'Your father's died,' and I was just sort of stunned. I had to go back in and give all my papers to Ian Mikado, and he said he would take over and I just went home. By this time they'd moved to London 'cos I couldn't look after them properly in Birmingham. It was like a dream, you know, you go in and he was lying in his bed in a slightly curved, very comfy, position. That was a lovely thing 'cos he had struggled so much with his breathing but he died in his sleep and he looked very comfortable. That was very important. I remember that. I still remember the image very strongly and then . . . I can't remember . . . all different members of the family were coming and obviously we had to organize the funeral and all that, and we must have done all that. I know we all just sat around and talked about Dad and drank some whisky and then for the next few days we talked about what the funeral was going to be like and obviously it was going to be a Catholic funeral. We had these kind of intense, but cautious, debates about which prayers we would choose and that was enormously important to all of us – that they reflected him. He was buried on St Patrick's Day which was brilliant, he would have loved that. So I think we got through those days by the organization of the process. That kind of gives you something to do that's all about honouring the person, but there's something practical also that you have to get on with.

*Do you think that those rituals are something which perhaps people don't do enough of?*

I think it's enormously important to have those rituals to reach for. And then there was things like my three little nephews taking the water and the wine up to the altar: having all the generations of the family. Ellie, one of my nieces, was just a baby then; she was in the church and that sense of a family and generations and somebody dying and a little baby still being his granddaughter, was ever so moving. And then the other thing we did: the seven of us, his daughters and his sons, carried the coffin and that was really important. I still remember it and I feel proud of it. It just symbolized there were all of us, and he was our father, and who else would it be? So having a ritual that we were all deeply familiar with, but within which you could make your own arrangements and choose your own prayers and symbolisms and hymns, was ever so important. Heaven knows what happens to people who don't believe in God; I think it will make it much more difficult for the people who arrange these things for us 'cos we haven't got the same sort of beautiful and moving rituals for those who aren't believers in God.

*Well, I was going to raise that with you because your parents were Catholic and you're a lapsed Catholic. Did you have any problem about those rituals because you didn't actually believe the essence of them?*

No, because I was very thoroughly brought up as a Catholic and I'm in no way anti-religious. There's lots of different world religions in my constituency and I respect them all and I broadly think that religion is a searching for goodness and for a moral in life both for oneself as an individual and for the global world. So I honour it and respect it. Every year, on St Patrick's Day, the whole family gets together and we go to that church to remember my father, and I don't go to Mass any other time; but I always go to Mass once a year.

*Do you think that would please him?*

It would please him that we all got together and it would delight him that it was St Patrick's Day!

*After his funeral was over, what were the effects on you? Did you have any physical response to his death?*

I think I went into a sort of slightly dreamy state. I had to carry on; I had to go to the Commons the next day. I did my Page Three Bill for the first time and got howled at. So I had to get on with my work but in myself I think I was in a sort of slightly dreamy state and there were things . . . like, I remember these blossom trees in Clapham, and I remember feeling their beauty more powerfully than ever. My dad loved nature and birds and so they would make me intensely think of him. I would think, 'Dad would love that blossom tree,' or just going along the road silly things like, 'Dad would think that,' and it wasn't like a sad tragedy. It was like I was very close to him, he was very close to me, and I was looking at the world with him and I think what I was proving to myself was that in one sense he wasn't dead. Because he was so in me in every way I looked at the world and in what I thought; he was still all around me.

One of my sisters was very upset; she was very close to Dad. I was trying to explain it to her, that you could do it this other way, that you didn't have to miss him. But she couldn't understand. She was angry that he was dead and I kept saying, 'But his body was worn out.' It did have to happen. I wasn't angry. I almost loved him more, and then it was this . . . delight. I really found out he is immortal for me. I mean, until I die he's part of my life and even now I sometimes think, 'What would you think of that Dad?' or, 'Wouldn't you like that, Dad?' He's in my life and I find that very lovely. I love it, and I'm surprised, and so he is immortal for me. That's lovely.

*Did you feel any need to take his place, say with regard to your mum?*

I think in the sense of her knowing that she's completely safe and the bills are paid – you know – I did that. I wanted her to feel one hundred per cent safe. But beyond that no. I mean, well, we sometimes talk about him. She lives with me in Birmingham, but I'm her daughter, not her husband. I suppose to be there for her, and see that she would never feel insecure or worried about money or anything like that – in that sense, I did feel the need to do that.

*Do you think the death of a parent in a way makes you more grown up?*

Absolutely. It made me mortal. Obviously I knew I was a human being and I would die one day, but once my father had died, I absolutely knew I would die. I became different. I knew that life was finite, and in that sense more serious – the remaining years that I had. I really knew that. I also felt deeply this paradox: that you have to have death for life to be life, that if life wasn't limited, if we were immortal, life would be completely boring and useless because you'd wake up every morning and say, 'I can do that in a million years.' It's the limitation on life that is part of its preciousness and intensity. That's my intellectual comfort; that's true, that's really intensely true.

*And you hadn't thought about that until his death?*

I may have thought of it intellectually but now I know it's very important. Anyone who's upset about death, I want to explain it to them. It is part of the beauty of life, and that's just the way it is.

*There's a quote I'm very fond of which I'll just put to you, by Colin Murray Parkes, who has written about and worked extensively with the bereaved. He writes, 'The pain of grief is just as much a part of life as the joy of love. It is perhaps the price we pay for love. The cost of commitment.' Do you feel that to be true?*

Absolutely. Because I mean, I always would have loved my dad but if he was still here and he was going to be here forever I wouldn't have known the preciousness and the intensity of it. None of us would reach the pinnacles of anything we do. Everything would be tedious and boring and repetitive in the end. We would become such useless things if we didn't die.

*When you express it like that it occurs to me that it is hard won. The way you described your father's death and your immediate feelings and the dreaminess and the sense of him in what he would have felt about nature – it sounds as if it was, with respect, easy for you. Were there*

*ever moments after that when you felt some of the negative grief that*
*your sister felt immediately?*

Not very much. I think Ann would accuse me of always trying to
turn things, but you see I did feel how much his body was
hurting him and one day he couldn't eat very much, and he was
very thin then, and I actually fed him some food and he ate a bit
more. And I thought, 'I should have done this before,' but in a
way I didn't want to; he always was such a dignified person. So I
think it was ready. He was ready; his body was ready. That's
different to someone who loses a young person or a child. I mean,
there was a niece of one of my aunts, a beautiful little girl . . . that
is much more difficult. But no, I didn't feel the rage. I felt the
loss, the bereftness, that he was gone. The empty chair – all that.
But I didn't feel angry.

*What was the attitude of the people who'd known them to his death and*
*to the family and to your mourning? Were they sympathetic, or did they*
*turn away as people do sometimes?*

Well, people say the Irish can deal with death. You show your
affection for those who are left and regard for the person who's
died. People say the British are very bad at it, but 'cos Dad died
in London we had the funeral in London, but then we had a
service in the local family church in Birmingham and it was
packed with people: Labour party, people Dad had talked with,
neighbours, black people, Asian people, Catholic people, Irish
people. And these different people paid their tributes to him and
it was very moving and very lovely. From the altar these different
people representing different parts of his life just made these
short tributes and everybody loved it and then we went to the
club and had a few drinks.

*Did you learn anything about him after he was dead that you hadn't*
*known?*

Well I still do. I was in a taxi the other week in Birmingham and the man said, 'You wouldn't have known this guy who taught me – Mr Short?' I said, 'Yes I do, he's my dad,' and he stopped the taxi in the middle of the road and started telling me stories. Now obviously what he was like when he was a young teacher I didn't know, so people tell you little stories and now I can't even remember what I knew before. It all fits together, you know, and I always go every year to Crossmaglen. I made this kind of commitment I wouldn't lose the family connection once Dad had died. And there's my aunts who are getting elderly and so on and they'll tell stories about when he was a little boy. Well obviously I didn't know those things but I just add them on to my sense of that human being.

*So in that sense is your picture of him still growing?*

Yes, but the core of it is the man I knew so well.

*What do you focus on when you think of him?*

I have this mental image of his face and I have this sense of his politics and his integrity and this sense of his love for nature – he loved birds, he loved seagulls and the sea – and it wafts . . . So I often refer to him in my mind about political questions or about big historical things 'cos he saw the world in those deep kind of profound ways, not just trivial. And I refer to him whenever I'm touched by the beauty of nature. He's there with me somewhere.

*You're a lapsed Catholic, but you're speaking in a totally Christian manner. What you say implies that you believe in an after-life, you believe that his spirit goes on?*

Well it does. He's still alive in me, but I don't believe in Heaven. I do believe we're all immortal in the sense that every single human being who has ever lived on this planet has left reverberations and scratches behind them, both in other people's memories of them in the consequences, good or bad, of the actions they took, and in the goodness they left in other people who loved them. In that sense we all reverberate forever and in that sense we're all immortal. I do believe that and my dad is present in that way. He is for me until I die, so he doesn't have to be in Heaven. I think that's just human beings yearning to place their affection for people somewhere, and also of course it comes out of human beings who had very difficult, hard, oppressed lives having a dream that at some time there would be happiness.

*And they would be reunited?*

Yes. I don't need that. I've got my own way of doing it.

*You feel you're perpetually united?*

Yes. It's not in an over-the-top way; it's all very kind of ordinary and that's just the way it is.

*Well you described him as a fine man, a good man – you're saying that goodness survives?*

Yes, and goodness is powerful because it centres there in you and my father was a man of enormous integrity. Not in any heavy way, but I would feel part of my honouring of him would be to try to have as good an integrity. Good strong influences – that's part of the immortality thing. They resonate on in other people. They help to make other people strong.

*Do you seek his approval still?*

Yes, but not in a kind of little-daughter-big-daddy sense. But thinking of this man that I so honour and admire and respect: I would like to be the kind of person that lives according to the values that cause me to give him that honour. Not seeking his approval but I'd show my respect by living according to the same sort of standards.

*Does your experience of his death equip you more to cope with so many of the negative things you experience as a politician? You mentioned being howled at in the House of Commons the day after your bereavement; in your constituency there's a lot of suffering: do you feel strengthened to cope with those things?*

I do in a way. Something so massive as the death of a parent you loved so much, puts some of the trivial pain that hurts at the time into perspective. Finally death is so absolute a thing that lots of the stupid little egos and vanities of politics recede. It's not good enough to live only on that level. One has to reach for something deeper and more profound and more important.

*Do you feel that the people around you, the people you meet, don't operate on that plane?*

Yes. But if anyone dies people write letters, you know, and it's so nice when people write and say how much they loved him. When you've just lost someone you love those letters. So I learnt that, and I always write to people when someone close to them has died; but whenever it's the first parent I try to tell them how monumentally significant it is. Do you know what I'm talking about? I had to be finally completely grown up and completely accept that I was mortal, and completely accept that I was totally in charge of my own life. I suppose I already was but in some way I moved on to a bigger thing.

*I just want to go back to something in the days and weeks after he died. Did you find it particularly hard because you were a public figure? You couldn't show your grief and you had to go on being a politician and doing all that that implies. Was that hard for you?*

No, it was funny. I had a particularly rough day the next day with the House of Commons at its most juvenile and revolting and I had a card from Neil Kinnock saying, 'Sorry about your dad and sorry they gave you such a hard time,' which I really liked. But I thought they didn't know what they were talking about. Their howling at me did hurt but maybe I could deal with it even better because I was involved in this profound thing. So their silliness was relatively inconsequential. It's funny, it's almost easier when you've got things you've got to do: you just do them, whereas if you've got nothing to do maybe it's harder to cope.

*But were there people who you showed your feelings to in the House of Commons? Did you have particular friends?*

I don't remember talking to many of them. It was a very family time. I wanted to get back to Mum and we would sit around and talk about Dad. I don't really remember. I know I did all the practical things: the Advice Bureau and the House of Commons and making speeches, and I remember this dreaminess, and I remember just going home and wanting to make sure Mum was alright and my sisters and so on. And talking about him a lot. That's all I remember really. So I did all the public duties perfectly practically and found I *could* do them all, but I don't remember wanting particularly to talk to people in that part of my life about Dad.

*Was it private?*

Yes, and precious. In politics people are always telling each other stories and everyone's always hoping the person will finish so they can cap it with their story. I didn't want to get into that kind of game-playing.

*Do you think it's important to people who are bereaved to talk about the dead person?*

I think it is. People do it in different ways, but I think the

buttoned-up-be-strong and avoid-the-tears-we-won't-talk attitude is wrong. I think you should cry and love and talk about it.
As the weeks and months went by I thought it important to talk
with my mum about how he wasn't a saint and that I remembered rows they'd had when I was little, 'cos I saw the warts too. I
said, 'Let's remember those things 'cos we're not going to pretend
anything about him.' You know, I think that's important too but
yes, you've got to talk and remember and laugh and cry and do
that with each other.

*In that process of remembering the warts side of it, did you ever think
about times when you'd been a beastly daughter to him and feel guilty
about that? Or maybe you weren't?*

Well, if I did things that would have upset him I don't feel
guilty. I don't feel guilty, I loved him. I was his daughter, and I
completely loved him and he knew that. I couldn't do any more
than that.

*Has your father's death affected how you've dealt with subsequent
deaths, or if not deaths, situations when people you love are seriously
ill?*

I think it's made me clear, not in a cloying way – and we always
were a close family – the big thing is that you've got to stay close
to the people you love and never neglect them, because you never
know what might happen. All you can ever do in the end is love
them and show your affection. If anything did happen and you
hadn't done it you'd never forgive yourself.

*Is that an ominous thought, if it lives with you? Is it a sort of
apocalyptic thought?*

That you're loving them in case you lose them rather than just
loving them because you love them?

*Yes.*

It probably is when I express it like that. I don't think about it like that. I don't *feel* gloomy about it. I am so pleased that I was so close to my father that I don't have any regrets, to some degree I want to be like that with everybody I love. Of course I do neglect some of my friends and I don't see everyone intensely all the time, but I do try.

*Your husband Alex Lyon has been very ill and you've nursed him. Is that almost more painful? Your father had such an easy death in the sense that although he'd been ill, in the end he died in his sleep and there wasn't a long period of suffering . . .*

Yes, well, Alex has Alzheimer's and it's very difficult because that means people aren't really themselves. There's still the body and the person but not the real person. He went into residential care in the summer. I found a lovely, caring, good place, but at Christmas he didn't know me, which I found very hurtful, and yet of course it's not his fault. In a way he's dead even though he's still alive because everything that was that person is gone. Except the remains; it's like being dead but the body hasn't died.

So that's very different, and much more painful. The process of being so ill is very corrosive. It's hard to remember the person as they were as it crumbles and crumbles and crumbles. With Alex, the only thing I can say – it's much more tragic and painful and awful – that I did do everything I could do. This is a much more unhappy thing, but it's given by the nature of the illness.

*So you can understand that some people do regard the death of loved ones as a relief?*

Oh yes. I don't know if one should think this, but I have thought that it would be better for him to die sooner rather than later because what he is now is not him. Obviously it's not up to me, but for him I would like that.

*Was the manner of your father's death important to you?*

Yes. That he wasn't. . . he'd been in hospital and that hadn't been very good. I'm really glad he wasn't in hospital; that he was at home; that he didn't have any kind of fit or a seizure, he just died and he was in this comfortable, curled position. That was just wonderful. So it was peaceful and natural. That was very lucky.

*When you describe him curled, almost like a baby – I'm thinking of when you said you fed him – was there any way in which you felt at the end that you were almost like a parent to him. That there was a reversal of roles?*

No. No, I was his daughter and I was helping to care for him. My mum was there, but he was very ill and needed a lot of care. But no, he was my father. He was the one; the big one. I was just the daughter.

*Just the daughter. That's interesting: that you see yourself as secondary to him.*

Well he was . . . the father comes first, you know. I don't know what it *is*: he was more important, more in charge. Even if he was vulnerable the roles never changed. I had quite a strong relationship with him: honest, and I'd tell him my views and all that, and he was living in my house. But he was still my father, the big father.

*Was he a better person than you?*

I try to be as good as him. In some ways yes; in some ways – he used to tell me about this – I'm warmer and more instantly affectionate to people. He knew that in himself. He used to say, about politics, 'It's always better if you can say it with a smile.' Not that I do, I'm not saying I implement that, but he wanted, partly, to be a more ebullient, warm person and he used to tell me I was lucky to have that. But I think he was probably more steely, more principled and absolutely un-selfseeking. I try to be like that, but I think he was more than I am.

# 11

# DANIEL TOPOLSKI

*Former coach of the Oxford Boat Race team, travel writer,*
*film maker and journalist, Daniel Topolski attempts to*
*encapsulate the spirit of his father, the artist Feliks*
*Topolski.*

*Can you describe your father's painting?*

Lots of lines. His drawings were always the raw material for the
paintings and there's this great sense of a drawing taking shape
on the page, terribly, terribly quickly. People were always
surprised at how quickly he was able to work. Many, many lines,
each one absolutely vital to the form of the picture. A great sort of
chaos of image appearing on the page. He recorded everything all
the time wherever he was: when he went to the theatre, if he went
into a restaurant or if he was in a war zone, he was drawing,
drawing, drawing. So there is a massive amount of terrific
reportage-type drawing. But for him, more and more, those
drawings became the raw material for his large paintings, and for
the last fourteen years his *Memoir of the Century*. It is a six-
hundred-foot long, twenty-foot high painting covering the
personalities and the events that he saw as forging the twentieth
century. At the same time for eighteen years he produced, every
two weeks, a broadsheet which he printed partly himself, partly
with some Polish friends of his. There was nothing he wasn't
interested in. And there are wonderful portraits of H.G. Wells, of
Stephen Spender, of Indira Gandhi, George Bernard Shaw, and so
on. Wonderful paintings. This unique body is so big and so

comprehensive, it is, I think, an unmatched artistic record of this century.

*Was the art like the man?*

Very much. A man of extraordinary breadth of interest. He was a journalist, he was a traveller, he was interested in everything and he ran with princes and kings and artists and beggars and really he covered the whole spectrum. He was never without a pad in his hand, drawing everything that he saw. Sometimes I'd drive him down a street slowly and at the end of the street everything that had been going on in that street was there on the page. So much better than a photographer because he had all those images on the one page, in the one drawing and then he'd come back and do the paintings . . .

He was brought up in Poland, born 1907, so he remembers as a seven year old the Cossack Horsemen riding through the town. He was sitting outside the back door doing his rather remarkable drawings, which still survive. Between the Wars he was studying in a little artists' colony just South of Warsaw; and that's where I want to actually set up a museum of his work in Poland. Then in 1935 he decided he wanted to see the rest of the world; he was in his early thirties and very well known in Poland. So he set off for Western Europe, spent some time in Paris but got very involved in London. Got a lot of work in London: *Picture Post*, *Night and Day*, there were a lot of journalistic periodicals that were very keen to have his work. And he did a lot of work for George Bernard Shaw designing sets and doing drawings that were used in some of his books, like *Pygmalion*. He was then taken on as a war artist and he was on every front during the Second World War. That really was the way his life operated. He wanted to be where the action was.

*Well having said that – and painting a picture as you've done of his tremendous energy – how did he cope with getting older and frailer?*

He just didn't accept it. Just didn't recognize it. His friends were teenagers as well as people his age and people older than him. He surrounded himself with energetic people. At his studio under the arches at Hungerford Bridge near Waterloo he had an open day on Fridays, so there would be this great trail of people coming through all the time: art students from Poland, actors rehearsing at the National, people from the States – a succession of people all mixing under this arch and all giving him great material for his work. During the Sixties and Seventies he used to have parties at the studio for all the punks and King's Road hippies.

*So he didn't accept getting old, because mentally obviously he wasn't ever going to be old. But there was a time, wasn't there, when he actually had to lean on you?*

There was a moment. He was a great traveller, as I've said, and I am too, and we hadn't really spent a lot of time together for a twenty-year period when he was in his sixties and I was travelling and busy with my life. We thought we should do a journey together and decided to go to South America; we would draw, we would write a book together, and the BBC were going to make a documentary about the trip. He was I guess seventy-five then and one of his great buddies, a fellow Polish artist said, 'Ah Feliks don't go, don't go to America with Daniel. He's trying to kill you!' Feliks was actually not all that well just before we left, and I thought he was trying to back out of the trip. It was going to be a big six-month trip right through South America: a journey around each other too, a sort of rediscovery of each other. Something I really wanted to do, and he did too. He was getting a little bit of trouble with diabetes and having some trouble with his left leg and there was a moment of possibility that he might not be able to come. I went on ahead, rather furious that he'd chickened. He joined me six weeks later in Chile, and we then continued this really quite gruelling journey: sixteen thousand feet over the High Andes and down along the Amazon. It was as we were getting to the Amazon that his leg and the diabetes started to give him a bit of trouble. And there came a moment when he was having to lean on me, when we were in some pretty difficult terrain. He would be leaning on me and holding me, and there was a moment when, in this television documentary, he says, 'I've finally come to the realization that I am less vigorous and that I am comfortable leaning on my son, and comfortable with oncoming old age.' Now this was at seventy-five, and for him it was a huge admission that he was no longer in competition, but he was content to settle back a little bit and relax within the context of father-son. And that was right. It all changed when he got home, I might add! He was back to his vigorous, independent ways. But there was a moment of acceptance there.

*Why do you use the word competition?*

I think there's always a sort of element of competition between father and son. He was very competitive always, very keen to show his vigour. He was proud of his energy, proud of his stream of ideas.

*Did you feel in competition with him because he was a famous artist?*

No. Luckily, I wasn't an artist or I think I might have had a bit of difficulty there. But I know there is this struggle of being overshadowed by a famous dad, and I don't think we ever had it because I went in a very different direction. I went into television and I was involved with rowing and coaching, and so there wasn't a sense that I was trying to compete or match him in any way. I remember when somebody said to him, 'Would you have liked Daniel to be an artist?' He said, 'No, I don't think so: he would have either been better than me or worse than me and I wouldn't have liked either of those possibilities.' So there was never pressure to go into the same field; I feel quite a lot of sympathy for children of politicians who go into politics or children of actors who feel they've got to act. But I think, you know, when parents are alive and vigorously leading their lives, and you are too, there's a long period where you don't really connect. And I think children tend to *waste* their parents a lot. They tend to waste the experience the parents have had. They kind of pooh-pooh it a little bit. And one really does regret it terribly afterwards.

*Were you like that yourself?*

Since he died I've regretted a lot that I didn't say. The same with my mother actually: I've regretted that I didn't spend more time talking. We talked a lot; and we lived together, for God's sake! We all lived together in the same house and we argued and talked all the time, but somehow I still feel a sense of loss for somebody I suppose I considered my best friend.

*That South American journey which was to be a voyage around your father, to quote John Mortimer's title, did it succeed? Did you discover things about him you didn't know?*

I did – but there are things I'm discovering about him since he died that I feel I ought to have known. I ought to have known that our name wasn't Topolski it was Tilpel, and that the name was changed to Topolski when my father was seven. I ought to have known that the family was Jewish and they became Protestant when he was seven. And somehow I didn't get these things.

*Was it because he didn't want to tell you or because you didn't bother to ask?*

I think he steered round it. He hated being typecast. He hated being pigeon-holed. It made it difficult for him as an artist because art critics found it difficult to pin him down. So there was always an element of mystery, of uncertainty, and when I was younger I didn't know the right questions to ask. I think people from middle Europe during and after the Second World War, find it very difficult to talk about that period. We've underestimated the suffering of people from that area, and I don't think they wanted to talk a lot about it. Now I think that's for a number of reasons, such as pretty atrocious experiences they didn't want to harp on. My father had left in 1935 so he wasn't a refugee as such, but he went back as a war artist and after, and I think there was also a sense of guilt at having survived when so many family and friends had died, had gone to concentration camps, had gone to war. I think there was a sense of not wanting really to confront it or to talk about it. Curiously, he wrote his autobiography, which was published a year before he died, and the first quarter of the big fat book covers the first forty years of his life and the other three quarters is the next forty years. So rather quickly that extraordinary period of history is dismissed. I've found now, talking to a lot of people of my age and kind of background, brought up here as English but of central European parents, we're all finding there's a gap, and we're being drawn back to Poland and Hungary and Czechoslovakia to find out more about our roots. So that's the biggest thing I miss: not being able to talk.

*Tell me about his death.*

I suppose one feels angry at a death. I mean, he was eighty-two. He was suffering from diabetes. He had a heart problem. Yes, he was vulnerable, but so vigorous and twenty ideas a day pouring out for work. And so it was difficult to come to terms with him being vulnerable and helpless. I didn't think that he was about to die; you know, you're not given any warning. He went into St Thomas's Hospital for some tests for the diabetes, just for some tests. But he was weak. I was trying to get the heart records from the other hospital which had been dealing with his heart problem. I went in to see him the day before he died and his room overlooked the Houses of Parliament. He said, 'I want some pencils tomorrow and some paper, 'cos I've got an idea for a mural that will involve the Houses of Parliament.' He'd always said that he wanted to die in mid-brush stroke, that he would be up on a ladder painting . . . So here was another part of his mural that he was going to do the raw material drawings for. So I said to him, 'We'll bring the pencils and we'll do it tomorrow.' Curiously I just wanted to ask him about his father, and I asked, 'How did my grandmother die? How did my grandfather die?' Completely inappropriate things to be asking, but I was not thinking that we were close to his death. And he said, 'Your grandfather was poisoned.' I found out later that he'd actually committed suicide and that was something again that Feliks wouldn't confront or face.

I left him that evening, and he had a heart attack in the middle of the night. We were called, got there too late, and the heart doctors were supposed to be coming in the next morning and I just felt it was . . . I felt angry that I hadn't been able to get the heart records from the other hospital and deliver them by hand. I felt that somehow something had gone wrong and it shouldn't have happened. I think that for someone who has somebody very close who dies much, much younger, that sense of injustice must be enormous. It's rather ridiculous for me to feel it when my father was eighty-two and very ill, but I still thought he had another ten years at least because his vigour proved it to me, and his mental agility. I just couldn't believe that he was ready to go, and of course it's nothing to do with whether you're ready to go: it's when they come to take you. It was a terrible shock. My mother had died three years earlier. That was a long drawn-out cancer death, and very painful, but you could see the whole thing happening. With my father: one minute he was planning his mural, and suddenly he'd gone.

*You mentioned that you were an emotional family. Did you cry when he died?*

Yes. Yes. I remember when my mother died the crying came a bit later. There were some tears, but I remember she died a week before the Boat Race, and my book was published at the same time, and I was going to do television programmes and stuff about the book. It was a ghastly two weeks and she died in the middle of all that. I did the Boat Race and then had to go straight to South America to Brazil with the crew. We were racing in Sao Paulo. And getting into a lift to go up to my room – it was one of these big kind of open-plan hotels with a glass lift going up the inside of the building – I was standing in that empty lift and suddenly I just completely collapsed in tears. Tears just flooding down. And it was the first time I'd been able to express that grief in that three weeks since my mother's death. With my father it was more immediate. There weren't other things happening as well, and I was able to feel it more. I was more at ease. I was angry, and there was a loss, and it had happened unexpectedly and, oh yes, I cried.

*Did you want to talk to people about him immediately? Was it important to you to communicate to people what you felt about him, or did you withdraw?*

I didn't feel an urge to talk, but I didn't feel an urge to withdraw. You know, there were the obituaries, and people 'phoned and asked questions, and I didn't feel I couldn't talk to anybody. Something that always amazes me is the parents of kidnapped children, or a child that's been abused or killed, on television talking about it. Almost immediately. I wonder how they can do that, but I suppose it's a way of wanting to get across the fact that this person was a person. You want people to know that this person existed and in a way you're trying to pinpoint. It might be shock as well: they can't think of any good reason to say no. But when a death actually happens I feel it does help to talk. I didn't feel I had to rush about babbling on but I was quite happy to talk to people about him.

*Do you think, as a society, we tend to push death away?*

Oh, we don't wail, do we? We don't wail, we don't scream and rant and tear our clothes . . . I think we really should sometimes. We do bottle it up and that causes us problems later. I'm sure we feel we've got to keep stiff upper lips and it's a bit embarrassing to show that emotion. We're a silly lot actually, the English, we really are very silly. We see it as a kind of weakness in others when they show grief or emotion.

*Do you think that's a particularly masculine thing?*

I think it's an English thing, but it's certainly a masculine thing: you know, men are not supposed to cry and one still has that. Little boys grow up believing we're not supposed to cry. We're supposed to be strong, like Daddy.

*Did you immediately have to organize everything? Did you have that sense of being the new head of the family and having to do everything?*

Yes – though we shared it, the three of us: this is my stepmother and my sister and I. We set up what we thought would be the sort of a funeral he would have liked. So there was no church. We went straight to the graveside in a horsedrawn carriage – big black horsedrawn carriage crossing the whole of Hampstead Heath, with wonderful girls in bowler hats and black outfits driving the horses. It was rather a glorious thing which held up all the traffic and caused a stir. He'd have liked that, I think.

*Was it something he'd ever talked about?*

Not really no. We'd buried my mother in Highgate Cemetery just six feet to the left of Karl Marx, which is where she stood politically. My father wasn't at all political and . . . Well he didn't really want to go in on top of her, he'd rather be sort of alongside her or somewhere else. That's about the only time I really ever talked about that. He may well have talked more to my stepmother.

*So this great ceremony that you invented – how did it come about?*

We just thought about it. We didn't think it was really appropriate that he should have a church ceremony, because he wasn't particularly religious: he wasn't an atheist, he was an agnostic. Everything for him as an artist, journalist – everything for him was being buffeted by events and observing and recording. He saw himself as a recorder of world events: he wasn't political, he wasn't religious, he wouldn't be definitive about what he believed. So to have a church ceremony was not quite appropriate but we wanted to somehow dress it – dress the funeral.

*Did his death change the way you thought of him at all?*

Not his death so much, but subsequently. I think that's part of the regret, you see, of realizing that he was a genius and that his work is quite extraordinary, and regretting that I hadn't really spent more time delving into his work, and delving into his life. I helped him with his autobiography, although he hated being edited. So I knew a lot about his life, and when I was very ill in hospital for a couple of months, he did come in religiously every day and found a way of passing the time where he started to tell me his life story. So each day was another chapter in his life story, which was wonderful, but which I didn't really properly remember and I just feel that I should have been more acute and more attentive during his life because I'm finding out since he died more and more what an extraordinary person he was. And going through his work all the time I am just astounded by the breadth and the talent.

*Obviously there were a great many obituaries after he died. Were they right? Did they sum him up correctly for you?*

I was pleased with them, and moved by them. I was moved by the mass of letters that came as well but, yes, there were certainly a number of those obituaries that did give him the recognition that was due. At the moment I'm trying very hard not to get sucked in and spend the rest of my life trying to do things on his behalf 'cos I've got my life to lead as well, but I do feel I want to try and get him better recognized and get his work better recognized and established over the next few years. He was so dismissive of the art establishment. It was only in the last six months of his life that he was made a Royal Academician and that was long overdue. He said he wasn't interested and that sort of thing, but he was secretly terribly pleased that that recognition had happened. He down-graded a little bit because he was so prolific, because they couldn't pigeon-hole him, because he didn't care about the establishment.

*Is there something particular in being the son – in as much as we've talked in this series about the deaths of parents of the opposite gender? Do you think it's particularly hard when your parent of the same gender dies, in that you're moving up, as it were, into their place? Are you conscious of that?*

Very. I think that nobody is going to love you unconditionally the way your parents do, so that's daunting. Suddenly there's no one now between you and death, so you're on the last lap, in many ways. We were very close as a family, very good friends. If I'd had to share a house with friends, I would have probably chosen my parents, although they split up late in life. Their opinions I respected, they were never obvious, they never had an expected reaction to a question. It would always be, particularly with my father, completely unclichéd, completely off the wall. I loved that and I don't know anybody else who can give me that. So I feel an enormous loss in that respect. But with a parent of the same sex . . . I mean we didn't have that close buddy-buddy relationship of talking about everything to each other. He wasn't my adviser on my social life or my sex life . . .

Until a parent or your parents die I think you feel immortal. You have this sense of everything *is*: there's no end to it, nothing's going to end. Suddenly they die and you're brought up with a start and you suddenly realize that you're on the treadmill and that it's going to end.

*You use the word 'treadmill'. Do you mean that his death made you more serious about life?*

I think it's a sort of mid-life crisis, probably. Up until then, for me life had every possible opportunity; you know, I was never going to die. I wanted to live until I was so old that I just had to be buried. There was always optimism; every day was great, and I had a great sense of living and travelling. Since then somehow, I've started to feel a sense of getting through it a bit, and a little bit of that ambition has been blunted, and a little bit of the energy has gone and . . . I don't quite know what. I don't think it was *just* his death. I think it was the fact that my mother died of cancer and then Feliks died, and then things I was very involved in came to an end. I mean the Boat Race business . . . I stopped doing that, and it had involved me for quite a long period. I wasn't quite sure where I was going from then. So there was a moment of questioning and uncertainty.

I've got two little girls now, and seeing my children arrive, I feel that my life is sort of being lived now through the children and my own life has now become secondary to the children's life; and I think all those things have combined in a rather uncomfortable moment, and that's why I say 'treadmill'. Because I suddenly feel that I'm having to earn a living now to support a family whereas before I was totally free to fly wherever I wanted to, to do whatever I wanted. I think that's overstating it, probably, but there's that sense that life is now less full of surprises, less full of spontaneity. I think I've emerged from it, but there was a moment when I felt quite low. A number of things, all highlighted by his death . . .

*Do you miss him now, as much as in the early days? How does grief change?*

I think it becomes a dull ache. You always miss, and there's not a day goes by when I don't think of both of them. But it becomes something you live with: it's just there. The ache and the missing becomes more remembering the nice things. The immediate loss is terrible and you just feel sorry for yourself. Later you think, 'God, how lucky I was to have such a great dad and a great mother; I mean, how lucky I was to have had such a good relationship with them for such a long time.' And I think it changes to fondness and warmth and good memories, and that replaces the anger and the loss.

*And that's there all the time?*

Oh yes. I have his pictures on the walls at home and my daughter loves painting. She's five now and we've got a little room set aside for her which is her studio, and she says, 'I'm going into my studio just like Feliks' . . . We're trying very hard not to push her in that way, but she does like her painting. And we all gather at his studio to keep the open day on Friday afternoons, for friends to come and see; and we'd like to keep the studio open much more, and I hope we will do if we can guarantee its security over the next few years. And going through all his work, that's a constant memory. It's a good feeling.

*You said that Feliks's death was a catalyst for you in the sense that after it you felt quite low about many things. You've also said that the positive side was this sense of remembering the happy things: how fortunate you were to have such wonderful parents, and of course, the work. Is there anything else positive that you learnt from his death?*

It's his energy and just his love of life, and love of adventure and his hatred of being channelled: that gives me a constant enthusiasm. I now feel vulnerable and mortal, and feel that there is limited time; and with that limited time I can take strength from all that *he* was able to achieve in his life. He never took no for an answer: everything was possible. He would bombard me with ideas for radio programmes and television programmes I should be involved in, of people I should be talking to, and books I should be writing. So not only was he full of ideas for his own work, he was full of ideas for everybody, and there was always a stream of people through the studio who were asking for him to pass judgement on their work, asking his advice about things. He really was somebody who enhanced a lot of people's lives, not just through his work but personally – he was a great fund of good advice and good feelings and good thought. His death has reminded me of how much he did during his life, and that really should reinvigorate me.

*And do you think that life-force never really dies?*

It didn't for him, and that probably gives one great hope. At eighty-two he was just packed with ideas right up until the last minute. And afterwards, the work. Just looking through the work, and seeing how much there was in the life, is a bit daunting because it makes you think, 'Well here's a life that produced a body of work that is going to live on forever,' and you think, 'Well, what the hell am I doing? I've written a couple of books, I've done a bit of coaching, I've produced two lovely girls, but what have I done? I've travelled a lot, but what have I done?' So it's daunting a little bit, if you actually think about it and worry about it. And I think . . . I would draw for myself the energy and the everyday love of living. That's what I'd draw from him.

# = 12 =

# TONY WHITEHEAD

*Tony Whitehead was the founder of the Terence Higgins Trust
and is now its President. He is currently Director of
Streetwise Youth Project, in London.
His partner George died of AIDS.*

I first met George in about 1979. I went with a friend to see a
play done by students; George was in the play and for some
reason we went backstage and we met him, and I couldn't stand
the man. I did not like this person at all. It was quite a few years
later, about 1985, when I met him again. A very different man
came to the Terence Higgins Trust where I was working, to help
with our education for drug users and HIV. I didn't realize at first
that it was the same man. I was deeply impressed by him.

*How had he changed?*

I learnt that he had been using drugs when I had met him the
first time and had quite a problem. It had apparently almost
killed him and he struggled very, very hard both to restore his
health and to kick the habit, and so that second time I met him
he was a very mature man, very caring and determined that the
experience he'd had as a drug addict was going to be turned to
value to help other people in that same situation. I was deeply
impressed with his strength and commitment.

Our relationship developed very, very quickly. I was alone at
that time: my life was almost entirely my work with the Terence
Higgins Trust quite early at the beginning of the AIDS epidemic

in this country. After about three or four meetings with George in the health education group that I was running, I asked him if he might like to come out to dinner and I made a joke of it, I said that it was important for new members of the Trust to come out to dinner with the boss which was not something which really happened. It took off very fast after that dinner, and within a week we were sharing my home and we just never parted from that day. It was very, very quick but very, very strong.

*And you loved him?*

Yes I loved him deeply. I was fascinated by him. I was impressed by him. I was made happy. There was a lot about George which really complemented me. I tend to be quite a serious sort of person; George had a great fun side to his nature. He would be very extrovert, he'd like to be in the public eye and I hated all of that – although my work at the Terence Higgins Trust demanded it at times. He was the perfect companion; he enabled me to get enjoyment out of situations like doing galas and making speeches. He was wonderful to be with. He was inspiring.

*When did you first discover that he had AIDS?*

George had never been one hundred per cent well, never particularly strong, when we started living together. In part, this had been the lingering effects of the problems he had had with drugs, and he was partially disabled and yet vigorous in his spirit. Then he seemed run down, and it seemed like an opportunity to have an HIV test. This would only be about six months after we had started living together. The test came back positive, which was a shock, but I had also, just about the time we met, been diagnosed as having HIV and so although it was a shock there was at least the feeling that, well, we were sharing a destiny to some extent, and there was some – not comfort – but some strength to be got from that experience. But whereas I was well, he kept on declining . . . A year after we were living together – I remember the day vividly because it was an important meeting for myself at the Department of Health in the afternoon – George and I had gone to the hospital in the morning. I was going to just drop him at home, thinking that there would be nothing too serious, and go on to this meeting which had the Chief Medical Officer and Sir Norman Fowler and all sorts of important people there. A policy discussion on AIDS. The doctor said that George had an AIDS diagnosis, because of some very serious infections which they had found, and he was to stay in hospital and start some kind of treatment. George insisted that I go on to the meeting and I remember sitting there in the Department of Health, kind of numb, and eventually it started to sink in and in the middle of this meeting with all these eminent people I just started crying. I just couldn't imagine what the next day or the next week or the next month was going to bring. I just couldn't see anything in the future except misery. I'd already seen people dying from AIDS, and I just thought, 'I can't, I can't, I can't handle this. I just can't handle this. I don't know what I'm going to do.'

*You knew all that time it was a certainty that he was going to die? There was no possibility of any reprieve?*

It's very difficult to give a definite prognosis with anyone with AIDS but the statistics and my experience of working with AIDS suggested that most people were going to die, especially then. Now with more sophisticated treatment it's a different picture, perhaps. Yes, we knew that he was going to die, but whether it was going to be a year, two, or three years we didn't know.

*How long was it?*

From being diagnosed to dying it was about three years in total, which was quite a long time. George was a real fighter. He had fought to overcome all the problems of his addictions and he was very, very strong; and I think that's why in spite of several times when I thought he was nigh unto death (as they say) he wasn't. It was three years and most of that time was pretty good.

*Did he experience despair?*

The negative side of that strength of character was that when it was impossible even for someone of such great heart to do the things he wanted to do, then it would be great despair. It would be so difficult even to get him out of bed. He wasn't so much giving up as just closing down, just trying not to think about it. Then perhaps some strength would return after a few days, but for someone of such determination not to be able to do things was terrible, and when he became progressively debilitated and disabled and walking became so difficult, it was terrible for him.

*Did you nurse him?*

George and I had talked a lot and very deeply about death and dying, as a kind of preparation for both of us. We made plans as to what he wanted to happen: he certainly did not want to die in hospital, and didn't want to be in hospital any more than was absolutely necessary. So although he would obviously have to go in for tests and treatment he would be at home most of the time and I would be with him. In the last year I gave up going into the Terence Higgins Trust and worked from home. I spent most of the last year with him, looking after him.

*It must have been a terrible burden on you from time to time. Did you ever resent it, even though you loved him?*

The feelings that you have for someone whom you love deeply who is dying or terribly ill and needs a lot of attention . . . I was deeply shocked and upset by the way I used to feel sometimes. I mean, I was expecting to feel sad or despairing or depressed at times, but I felt sometimes angry, bitter, resentful: really negative feelings which I was ashamed of, and which I tried to pretend I wasn't feeling. So angry with him, as though it was his fault that my life was being, or as I saw it then, spoilt. Everything was ruined, everything was lost. It wasn't just because I was giving up fulfilling work, it was because I was losing him and I was blaming him for that. It was because the man whom I had fallen in love with was going before my eyes; it wasn't just a case of when he dies he's gone but before that. A person changes. There was a time when in addition to all the physical problems of the disease he became very severely mentally ill and developed a kind of paranoid psychosis which was perhaps the most distressing part. At least with a physical illness the spirit is still recognizable, but with a psychiatric illness of this kind it's the spirit which changes. He would accuse me of doing the most terrible things. At one point he began to think that he was talking with God and would proclaim what God was saying to him about me. There may be times when anyone in a situation like this is going to be offhand or a bit short-tempered, but this was way beyond that; he was accusing me of going out in the middle of the night to murder people, and crazy things. It took a long time for me to really realize that this was beyond normal even for someone who was dying, and to actually persuade him to get proper psychiatric treatment. He had to be hospitalized for that. He was terrified that his mother and myself were cooking up some plan to have him locked away in hospital; he was just terrified, absolutely terrified. Thank God, the hospital were wonderful and they managed to sort a lot of this out and the man I knew was restored to us. It would be about nine months after that he died, so we had a chance to really be together again, even though he was so ill.

*You mentioned Goerge's mother . . . I was wondering about family and friends and what kind of support you both had. Were people sympathetic?*

George had been somewhat alienated from his family. He loved them, but when they were together there would be problems very quickly. It was a complicated relationship with his family.

*Do you think it might have been because he was gay: they couldn't accept that?*

I think him having been gay had been a problem but also what he had put them through when he was a drug addict. His family finds it difficult to handle feelings, and the feelings of losing your son are painful in the extreme. It was difficult for his mother particularly, and for his father, and for him to express themselves without the pain getting in the way of what it was they really wanted to say to each other. So there were some very difficult times. I worked quite hard with George to enable a sort of reconciliation with his mother because I just knew that it was going to be important for both of them. In a way it was important for me too because his mother and I became a support to each other. And eventually, at the very end when he was dying, his mother came to stay in our flat. It was only about a week but I was very glad that she was there.

*And so you both looked after him at the end?*

At the end, yes.

*Did that please him? Was he aware of the significance of that?*

I think that was terribly important to him. What had happened was he had gone into a hospice for respite care, so that I could have a break. At this time he was very ill; the doctors said he would die within weeks or months. I felt bad about not having him there, but one gets into the situation where you're just desperate, not to be away from the person you love, but for a break. This was a wonderful, wonderful hospice and when he was in there he developed a brain infection and became very quickly very ill. His mother and I were with him a lot of the time and he had said, 'Just get me home, get me home.' The people at the hospice moved heaven and earth to get us home and I remember it was in the middle of one of the transport strikes that London had a few years ago, and we had the ambulance, and it was just terrible trying to get through the traffic to get him home quickly and in comfort. His mother stayed with us then because we knew it wouldn't be very long. Because of the brain infection he was not really able to speak very much, and I don't remember him ever calling for his mother before but I think that night or the next night he did call for his mother. And she was there and that was so important. I don't know what I would have done if she hadn't been and I couldn't have got her there. It was important for him and it was terribly important for her.

*You said that you and George had talked a lot about death together in the early stages. How did you approach the actual event?*

George had made it very clear to me, to his friends, to his family, that he did not want to be allowed to linger in pain and distress, that he wanted help to end his life at a time he believed to be appropriate. It was very easy to agree with that when he was well; when the prospect seemed a long way off; when the promise from myself that I would do whatever was necessary to help him gave him a lot of comfort. The idea that he was going to lie there disabled, incontinent and confused was terrifying to him. When we got home from the hospice and he was then so ill, I began to be very afraid. Was he going to die easily or was he going to face the very thing he'd been afraid of? We spent a lot of time together but he was hardly able to talk. Then one night – we still shared a bed even though he was so ill because I didn't want to be apart from him – his mother was sleeping in the front room, and we had a nurse on night duty out in the corridor outside the bedroom; the house was so full, and somehow night was the best time because he would perhaps be a little more lucid in the early hours. He just gently squeezed my hand and said, 'Please, help me, please help me,' and I knew what he was talking about. So I just screwed up my courage – maybe I was frightened – and said, 'Yes, I promised and I will,' and he said, 'Thank you,' and that was the very last thing he said to me; he was not able to speak again.

The next day there seemed to be so many people in the house: doctors coming in, nurses coming in, family coming in. With the help of a friend I managed to get everybody out of the house, and we had . . . we had made our plans. He had said what he wanted to happen towards the end. It was a lovely, lovely summer's day – 1989 – it was such a beautiful summer and I could hear children playing outside and the windows were open, the breeze was coming in, and we did what we had planned. And I just held him and he died just as he had hoped, gently – just, just, slipped away in my arms. In retrospect, I don't know if I could have lived with myself had I not helped him to do what he had decided when he was well and rational. I'm very, very glad now that I did do as he wished, as we had decided. And that we were together and it was peaceful and not painful.

After about half an hour everybody came back from the shops, and as you can imagine all hell broke loose. It was terrible. It was absolutely terrible. I think his mother had feared this was what was going to happen. She knew, she knew. George had been very explicit that he wanted to be helped to die if death didn't come easily, and she had been afraid of this and according to my friend who had taken her shopping, she practically ran the last hundred yards home. Because she just knew in her heart.

*What was her response to you?*

She was at that time deeply angry that in a sense I had stolen from her his last moments. I do feel very sad about that, because I do feel very strongly for her how painful to have lost those last moments. But the truth is, it had to be just the two of us, had to be just the way he had wanted it. After days, weeks, we were able to talk about it and eventually she thanked me, and she realized that it just had to happen the way it did. It was, in a sense, fortunate that he and I were able to be together in those minutes and after he had died. I was just sitting on the bed holding him; it was a kind of calm; the peace that he had got in dying just kind of filled the house. That just evaporated the minute his mother came back. I will never ever forget the cry that she let out when she held him. It was the pain of a mother losing her child: something that just filled the whole world. And that calm that I had found when he and I had been together went. All my pain just came out as well.

I left her with him, and the plans for his death had also included that he did not want to be taken out of the house immediately by an undertaker. He wanted me to wash him and to lay out the body, and where I come from that was quite traditional. There would be someone in the village who would come and help with the body and the body would stay in the house. This is what we did. I washed him, with the nurse, and laid him out properly and dressed him in the clothes he wanted and stripped the bed and laid him down in clean sheets. And he looked beautiful, I mean, he really looked beautiful. He stayed in the house all that night, and the rest of his family would come in and spend time with him in the bedroom, and his very closest friends would also come in and stay there in the bedroom, and we were all together all through the night, and then the undertakers came and took him next morning.

*Do you think there's comfort in those old-fashioned rituals?*

For me and for his friends and for his family it was terribly important that we did things in the way we did. I was doing the last things that I could do for him. Also to be able to spend time with his body in that way . . . it was not morbid at all. He was no longer in pain and you could see it. His features relaxed when he died and he looked like he was sleeping. It was very important just to be able to spend time with him and perhaps to say things to him that you seem not to have had time to say before. I couldn't imagine what it would be like had he died in hospital or been whisked away very quickly after he'd died. I think the way so many people approach death today . . . well, I can't say it's wrong, it just doesn't seem appropriate to want to tidy them away like that. The life had left his body but he was still there.

*How did people cope with your grief, two or three months afterwards?*

I had a very difficult time after George died. Very difficult. I'd always been so capable and so strong but I don't think I was prepared for the misery that followed. I don't think my friends were really prepared for what I was going through. In the first few days, even in the first few weeks, people were very, very good. I was never alone and there was so much to do: the funeral to arrange – all those sort of details. There were people to contact. There were letters of consolation which were very beautiful. I had been writing a regular health column, and obviously it had come to feature a lot about George and the death. From people I never knew I got letters and there was consolation in that, and there was also just the work of trying to answer them and deal with people. I suppose it was months rather than weeks afterwards, when it was painful and people's lives seemed to resume and mine didn't. There just seemed to be nothing. It was very frightening. I remember one day, about two months after George died, I was just coming back from the shops, in my own street, about a hundred yards from where I lived, and suddenly I was lost. I didn't know where I was; I was completely lost. I was frightened. I started crying in the street. It was just as though I'd been taken to another place and dropped: completely unfamiliar. In a sense, physically being lost in the street was paralleled by being lost in my life. I suddenly didn't know what I was doing. It was as though for so long everything about my life had been focused on George and that had gone and there was just nothing.

*Do you think that the world was as understanding of a bereavement like yours as it would have been had it involved a 'normal' married couple?*

Many people are uncomfortable or ignorant about the nature of a relationship between two men or between two women, given that it's hard to recognize and appreciate what the relationship is, and extremely hard to recognize and appreciate what the loss of that relationship would be. Having said that, I was fortunate that my friends and my family and his family were very supportive of my loss, and they understood that in matters of the heart and the spirit the sex of the people involved has absolutely nothing to do with it. And my neighbours in the same house understood that simple truth, and were kind and considerate. But I've known people in that situation who have not been able to acknowledge their grief to anybody because they're so isolated. I'm deeply, deeply grateful to my family and so impressed by my parents who have had problems about the nature of my sexuality and my relationship with George. But I was not quite aware of the depth of their maturity and their love, until they helped me when he died. I'm deeply grateful for that and always shall be. I couldn't imagine what it would be like had I not been able just to express my grief when I needed to. There was consolation in that. I mean I don't think in those painful weeks, months, that follow the loss of someone you love anything really makes it feel better. No matter how wonderful the people around you are, the experience is still a deeply lonely experience. To lose someone you love is also to lose a whole way of life, to lose a great part of yourself and that is always going to be a lonely journey. You gradually resume life, rediscover yourself, begin to find pleasure in life again . . . but you'll always have to do that alone.

*Do you feel guilty when you start to rediscover pleasure? Is there a sense of betrayal when you pick up the pieces very slowly?*

There were times when slowly you find consolation in something unexpected. I mean a lot of the things that people think are going to make you feel better – kind words and sympathy – one appreciates but it doesn't actually do a lot. The things I enjoy are very much to do with gardens and nature and all that kind of thing, and perhaps I'd be walking along and the sight of something growing would suddenly bring a sort of comfort. And I'd be quite surprised: 'My goodness, I'm actually feeling something good here.' I don't think one felt guilty about little things like that which so unexpectedly brought some sense of pleasure, some sense of life continuing. It was quite a long time, but when I actually started trying to go out again, to deliberately socialize with people, to go dancing or to the theatre or something – that was difficult. And to start meeting new people, as opposed to old friends: people who didn't really know about what had happened – that would be difficult, and would make me feel confused; almost as though I wanted to let go of the pain I'd felt, and yet felt I shouldn't let go, that it would be to betray George and what we'd been to each other.

*You and George talked a lot about death, as you've said. Did that make you think about your own death?*

Inevitably. On the one hand, although I'm quite well, having HIV does statistically increase my chances of dying. And the experience I've had of other people has been that when one person's died of AIDS, it's often not been long before their partner has died also. So in that sense it was very understandable that one would think about death. Also the experience of George's death has had a lasting legacy: it's made me somewhat less afraid of dying. I don't think about it all the time; my life is very fulfilling now. But having seen death: it's not quite so frightening. An imagined enemy I think must be much more terrifying than an enemy that you have met, however terrible that enemy is. I mean, there's nothing to be afraid of; although leaving life behind is something that I don't want to happen. I love life. But I hope that when (and I hope it's a very long time away) my time comes I will be able to meet death with something of George's calmness and courage. He gave me lots and lots of things in my life, and the last thing he gave me was this feeling of calm and courage about when the time comes to die.

*Because there's still a lot of public ignorance about AIDS, and prejudice against the sufferers, does it make it worse for you when you read about a showbiz death, see all the tabloid attention?*

The way the media tend to deal with death from AIDS makes me extremely angry, because they focus on sensationalism, because of their obsessive interest in how they think a person actually contracted the disease and because of the kind of blame which they wish to apportion to people who have died of AIDS. I've become extremely angry because they simply don't recognize that this is a human being dying. In the cases that make the papers – you know, stars and singers – they're human beings who've actually given a lot to the world. Human life is worth much more than some balance sheet of the causes of their death. It's almost as though they're trying to take away that person's humanity, and that the experience of death, which is one thing which we will all face and which should, like birth, unite us all, is being used as something divisive by the media when discussing AIDS and HIV. People have this idea that AIDS is a self-inflicted disease, when so many illnesses may be self inflicted: smoking-related diseases, people who play dangerous sports, etcetera. People have to live their lives in a way which is meaningful and fulfilling for them; the greatest crime is not to live your life very fully and perhaps sometimes suffer the consequences of a very full life, which may be a premature death. George's life was in many respects very fulfilled, and a life which meant a lot to other people. That's what's important, not the nasty sniping about the number of sexual partners a certain singer had. That's atrocious.

*How do you remember George now?*

Mostly when I think of George I think of good times, good things. I'll often suddenly find myself smiling as I remember something he did at a party, or when we were on holiday. There were very funny times, even when he was terribly ill. When I'm travelling now, I remember the difficulty we'd have with

George's medicines: trying to travel to places for our holidays and having to smuggle the medicines. We would fill suntan lotion bottles because of the concern that if this customs person wherever we were going found that he was a person with AIDS we might not be let into the country. So most of the time I remember George very positively, he brings a smile to me. Sometimes, sometimes, you can be lying in bed or very quiet, and a vision of him being very, very ill or his death will come into my mind, which is still deeply shocking. I mean, I'll sit and think long and happily about the good times but I won't sit and deliberately think about the bad times and his death; and it's only when I have to do it, such as now, that I put myself through that experience. I actually try to shut it out, to close the door on it.

*But the door never really closes does it?*

The door never really closes and there's always a crack there and it blows open unwanted and unasked for. In a sense, as I said earlier, there is something positive even in an experience of such sadness, something that one can take from that. One can learn it's a little foolish to try and shut it out anyway. You have to accept that you've been through this experience and nothing will ever replace the loss, and you can't really shut it out. For me, I don't suppose I really want to: I've learnt from it and I've benefited from it. George has given me something, and made me a wiser person.

# Appendix

Twelve people chose to share their experiences with me, and in doing so shared memories, grief and love with many listeners to Radio 4. Usually in these circumstances the interviewer remains a cipher – the catalyst in a conversation, maybe, not an equal participant. Yet when I wrote privately to all these people, asking them to participate in the series, I felt it important that they should know the source of my own interest in the subject of death. This book would not be complete, therefore, without an account of a particular bereavement, which wrenched me into a meditation upon death in a way that sadness at the loss of my grandparents had not done. *'I had seen birth and death but had thought they were different. . .'* (T.S. Eliot, 'The Journey of the Magi').

The first article appeared in the *Guardian* in January 1976, but was in fact written one week after the stillbirth of my second son. It aroused an extraordinary, moving response from readers, an avalanche of letters which I still have. The second article appeared in the *Listener* in November 1985, and was the one I sent to those invited to give their 'perspective for living'.

## 26 November 1975

I remembered pushing, breathing through a mouth like the Sahara. Then at five am I regained consciousness in my small cubicle, staring confusedly at the dim red light they leave burning in the rooms of the sick, wondering what had happened. Needing a bedpan I groped stiffly for the bell, brain clearing, awareness dawning. By the time the nurse came I knew – though my hand still felt my stomach to see if he was still there. 'What happened?' I asked. She looked distressed: 'Don't you know? You had your baby and it was a little boy . . . and he isn't alive.'

For three hours, until my husband came, I could not cry. They had taken me into hospital two weeks earlier to rest because of my lack of weight; they had induced the birth three weeks early in a (now I see) desperate attempt to prevent his inevitable death inside me; the night before the labour I rang a friend and said I was convinced my baby would die. But such is the gap between what the heart hopes and the mind knows, that I could not take in the fate I had predicted. During sixteen hours of awful pain, made worse by the anxiety, I hoped he would live, I expected him to live, I laboured for his life. Now my husband and I were left to weep in each other's arms – like all parents of stillborn babies devastated by the extent of the love and loss we felt for someone we had never met.

The following days taught me more about the nature of motherhood – as well as of suffering – than did the birth of my first son, Daniel, who is now two. The gap ached – so much so that one sleepless tormented night I tiptoed downstairs to get Daniel's teddy bear to take back to bed: the vacancy in the womb had been replaced by an emptiness in my arms and some small thing, anything, was necessary to fill it (and they send women to prison for stealing babies).

On the fourth day after the birth-death I awoke to find my breasts full of milk – nature's cruellest irony – ready to feed the baby who was not there. Like a full cow past milking time, I cried. And like an animal I could not understand: all the intellectual/feminist debate on the nature of motherhood and the needs of the family dissolved beside the awfulness of the physical loss, and need. For nine months I had been prepared for a baby. Without that baby I was still a mother, ready, and cheated. When I cried bitterly three nights in succession that I hated being a woman, hated being married, hated being trapped, I was expressing an awareness more fundamental than that of my role, more an unwilling acceptance of my function.

He was born and died on the Wednesday. On Friday I was discharged from the hospital – the doctors and nurses, though kind and upset, were unable (I sensed) to cope. Out of place amidst waiting pregnant women, and the mewls of the newborn, and post-natally depressed girls staring helplessly into metal cots full of responsibility, had come death, and it was an intrusion. Some mothers of stillborn babies want to see and hold their dead baby, though I did not. But significantly, it was never suggested. Those who have escaped the experience cannot approach its meaning: that a stillborn child is a real person to the mother (and father, in this case) who bore him/her.

One day at home a friend rang, and I heard my mother say, 'Bel lost her baby.' The euphemism outraged me. For I did not lose him like an umbrella or a lover. He was born and died. To be accurate he was born dead: the ultimate contradiction in terms, so mysterious it defies analysis. When I heard that acquaintances thought I had miscarried I was equally outraged – it seemed important that they should realize the gulf between that sad accident and what we had been through.

That gulf is symbolized most clearly by the requirements of bureaucracy: the fact that my husband had to go, one bleak rainy day, to get a piece of paper from the hospital, then go to the Registrar's office and 'give the particulars' – all written out in laborious longhand in the special book for the Stillbirths that are neither Birth nor Death, but both – then return to the hospital with another piece of paper to discuss funerals, prices, whether the ending would be Christian. Though we did not attend the plain cremation the state requires and provides it was strangely consoling to think of him in his shroud and tiny, named, doll's coffin. 'Fitting' is the word: that a life which had begun should be ended with some rudimentary ceremony. Afterwards, people rang. I wanted to tell the story: to talk about him gave his brief life a meaning, to share the experience with others gave it importance. Morbid it might (superficially) seem, but it was necessary: an exorcism of pain that was also a sharing of love.

Those who have experienced the death of a baby probably feel first (after the tears) the need to blame. In this case first occurred the possibility that the hospital could have done something. But doctors are not gods, nor is science without its limitations. We assume that the process of pregnancy and birth is without its old perils – though still something like twenty in a thousand babies die. When your baby dies you look at loaded carry-cots with new wonder, the leap into the world seeming all the more perilous. All that ultrasound equipment, all the knowledge of obstetrics . . . and the doctors, doing all they could, were blameless.

But needing to find a reason, you turn upon yourself. I knew that I had rested as much as I could and eaten well – I had stopped work and cooked nourishing meals of liver and greens. I did not want simply to make him grow. But blame lies deeper. The day after his birth-death I raved at my husband like a child: 'I haven't been wicked. I've tried to be good to people . . . I've been a bit wicked but not that wicked.' The words assumed an area of responsibility far deeper than the physical, more primitive and necessary than sleep or food. I blamed myself in two ways. I felt that I had failed as a woman, in that I had not managed to fulfil the sexual function I had assumed (either by conditioning, or by instinct) as my own. More important, I assumed I had failed as a person: somehow I had 'gone wrong' and so I was being punished.

By whom? One day a woman who happens to be Catholic visited me at home, and when I explained to her how real that baby seems, and how I am conscious of having borne two sons, she said: 'You realize you are talking in a religious way?' Of course I did. Though an agnostic I was, for lack of anyone else, blaming God for my son's death.

He was born at midnight, though they stopped (unknown to me) listening for his heart at 10.20 pm. That was 26 November 1975, his birthday. On the 27th I heard myself asking my husband if our baby had a soul – and where had he gone? A friend who had the same experience told me that it made her leave the Catholic Church: she was told that her baby, unbaptized, had gone to Limbo, that terrible empty place they reserve for children who have died without sin, but whose original sin, unredeemed by baptism, has denied them Heaven.

But I discovered, after initial grief and subsequent bitterness and rage, that I do not believe in original sin – just in original goodness. As we shared sorrow my husband consoled me by saying that his own comfort lay in the conviction that his baby died pure – he was conceived, and existed, and died. It was simply a speeding-up of the process we all experience, without the pain, without the regrets, without the hurting of other people, without the sickening consciousness of universal misery, without the disappointments of age. Also, of course, without the moments of joy – but then, he was wanted, cherished, loved, and so in that there is a joy he might have felt. How do we know what the unborn feel?

Without any joy to wipe out the memory I keep remembering the labour and see myself as through the wrong end of a telescope – a creature on a bed, writhing, vomiting, crying, almost unable to bear the physical suffering. Afterwards, longing for my baby to cuddle, I see myself railing at my husband, almost unable to bear the mental anguish. But it is in that 'almost' that the majesty lies. Because we do bear it, and we still want to live; all the love and hope and pain and loss, the resilience and acceptance, are all the more precious because of the darkness that surrounds them.

Five days after I came home I received a letter from man called George Thatcher, a talented playwright, serving life for murder in Gartree for a crime he steadfastly maintains he did not commit, and who cannot obtain parole. I had written an article about his case, and he had been told about my baby, by a mutual acquaintance.

His letter began: 'I'm not going to make you cry because you have shed enough tears. But somewhere along the line there is a joy for you which will surpass all that pain – and only be possible because of it.' That sentiment – expressed (ironically enough) by someone who after thirteen years is still deemed unfit to rejoin society – brought the most comfort, identifying the one thing that, for us, gave our baby's brief existence purpose. There is no divine right to happiness, simply a duty to cope, to understand, and to love. My duty to my first son seems clear and easy; but there is also a duty to that second baby.

I do not wish to 'get over' his loss, nor do I wish to replace him with more children. I simply wish that his life and death should be absorbed into my own: enlarging, and deepening in perception.

## The Spirit Cannot Die

Speech after long silence – I find myself driven to return to a subject I thought I had left behind. The compulsion has much to do with the time of year: November, with its damp leaves, wind and desolation and the sense of falling forward into darkness. With this comes an unavoidable sense of anniversary. For thought I may attempt to deflect, and to keep at bay through frantic activity, it is impossible to avoid remembering something which happened ten years ago this month. Defiantly, I wonder why I should thus apologize for the fact, to myself as well as to you. So – no apologies. It happened. It was a death: a very small death, but a death for all that.

For it was in November 1975, after fifteen hours of labour and at full term, that my second son was born dead. Not long afterwards I wrote about the event for the *Guardian*, an article which had an astonishing effect. Letters flooded in from those who had also suffered this strange and (then) unspoken-of bereavement, which is birth and death in one. As a direct result of that readers' response an organization called the Stillbirth Association was formed, which still flourishes; later, the Health Education Council published a booklet; slowly, attitudes began to change and hospital staff showed a much greater understanding . . . But none of that concerns me now. All of it was a long time ago, but there is still something left to set down: that all of us, in our understandable and selfish terror, underestimate the capacity of death to have a profound, positive and lasting effect on life itself.

Let me say hastily that it is not large-scale death of which I speak, not the result of war, famine, catastrophe or outrage, but the simple, ordinary, individual death which each one of us has to confront – sooner or later. Though each death will be different and experienced in raw freshness each time (the death of a child, the death of a friend, the death of a beloved parent), the first response is usually anger – a railing against the heavens for allowing this to happen. It would be astonishing were that not so.

When (for example) a distinguished man dies at the 'early' age of forty-eight, after courageously fighting a terrible illness for several years – a man at the height of his powers with a great future cut short and a wife and two growing children left bereft, then any of his friends will hear of his death with impotent rage. Why should such a man lie dead when all around the mean, the idle, the corrupt, the inadequate, the ignorant, the brutal, thrive in their health and strength? Each day, somewhere, somebody reiterates Lear's long scream of agony at the unfair absurdity of it: 'Why should a horse, a dog, a rat, have life, and thou no breath at all?'

Close cousin to such indignant pity for the dead is the understandable self-pitying questions of those left behind: 'Why *me*? What have *I* done to deserve this?' There is no answer to either cry. Yet we can stumble towards a 'hint half understood' by means of one simple, yet devastating and demanding exercise. Instead of 'Why?', turn the question on its head, and ask 'Why not?' That is the essence, the mystery.

For although you may hate the fact of death, you can still, simultaneously, accept that it has to be; it is also possible to take this a step further – going beyond mere passive acceptance, and seeking instead to discover what results from the pain. Fear is the first thing – and it might as well be accorded full import. *Timor mortis conturbat me*, uniting us with those medieval men who were terrified into living virtuously by the vision of the death's head: the prospect of worms eating the body, hellfire devouring the soul. Now – when the fire consumes the body and there is only vacancy for the soul – the fear is worse. A recent article by the novelist A.N. Wilson (published in the *Spectator*) seemed to me to be evidence of this. In a straight-talking attempt to be strong-minded, to confront the 'facts of death', it confused nervous, schoolboyish callowness with honesty – symbolized most jarringly by the repeated use of the word 'stiffs', for dead bodies. It was about the pathology of death – only one infinitesimal part of its mystery and truth; and it was suffused with revulsion and horror.

All my life, *until* my child was stillborn, I would have shared that fear, and shouted with rage against the 'dying of the light'. I would quote, with approval, Simone de Beauvoir's words: 'There is no such thing as a natural death: nothing that happens to aman is ever natural since his presence calls the world into question. All men must die; but for every man his death is an accident, and even if he knows it and consents to it, an unjustifiable violation.'

Now . . . I am not so sure about the truth of that stirring arrogance. It may serve to explain the courage of the dying, but is there not a danger that it also explains it away? An even more familiar and over-quoted phrase is also perturbing: 'Any man's death diminishes me.' Donne's great meditation still reaches out across centuries with its plea for fellowship, for compassion. Yet it, too, may be questioned. Why should any man's death necessarily diminish? To witness a death borne courageously, to read of heroism and death in the face of persecution . . . does that not *enhance*? There is a serious case for saying that every man's death adds to me, if I allow it; and far from being a violation, death may be a consummation – although not devoutly wished. To put it another way: it is life that we diminish by turning away in such horror from its ending, for (in Jung's phrase) waxing and waning are part of the same curve.

I know no greater expression of this idea than Schubert's String Quartet in D minor, known as 'Death and the Maiden'. Schubert, fated to live the pitifully small span of thirty-one years, leaving works of beauty and majesty unfinished, not even having had the chance to hear most of his chamber music performed – Schubert understood death even before it came. In the song *'Der Tod und Madchen'* the young girl is appalled to find death near, saying she is not ready for him. The reply of the Reaper is tender: 'Be of good courage, I am not wild, you will slumber gently in my arms.'

In the variations on these bars in the Quartet, we can hear the eternal dialogue plainly. It is like someone walking out into the deep, feeling the undertow pull, the swell of death start to lift and carry away, only to turn for a moment and scrabble wildly in the direction of the departing shores of life . . . before turning back and accepting the end. The final mood is not tragic, but relentlessly exciting – as though by turning to face the spectre face to face we see, for the first time in that dreaded visage, a strength and a sweetness which we recognize proudly as our own. What we were born to.

Coming to terms with the idea of one's own death is hard but essential; only then is it possible to contemplate with any equanimity the death of those one loves. And I would interrupt all the wise phrases of bereavement counselling, all the talk of 'loss', with this blunt truth: that when someone you love dies you might as well accept the fact that you will be haunted by that person for the rest of your life. A proper *haunting* – that is what I have known for ten years, but have only just realized. Each year at this time, I have imagined my baby growing, changing, experiencing the stages of school, friendship, fun – a vision that is in stark contrast to the reality: the cremation I did not attend, and the ashes I never saw scattered on rosebushes. That is not morbid; it simply invested what happened with permanent dignity. And nor do I mind it any more – 'the third who walks always beside' . . . because without the sum total of ten years' imagining I would certainly be the lesser person.

It is a blithe spirit indeed, and I do not want it exorcised. From corpses and 'stiffs', through spooks and ghosts, we arrive in the land of spirits, and that linguistic journey is a lesson in reverence and lack of fear. It involves a willingness to love the dead for what they are – the *Manes*, the souls of the departed, for whom we go on living, doing all the things they could not do, and allowing them to add to the whole of what *we* are.

In the multiplicity of grief I do not compare mine with that of parents I have met at Great Ormond Street Hospital, or the widow of the man cut down in his prime. Yet all of us – angry, demented, guilty, bitter, released, disappointed or however we may respond – have this in common: we are placed permanently on the interface between suffering and acceptance, and weighed with the knowledge that death is simultaneously an individual agony and the most unarguable testimony to ordinary, sublime humanity. The grief goes on – and there is a very good reason for this permanence. In the words of Franz Marc: 'The spirit cannot die – in no circumstances, under no torment, despite whatever calumnies, in no bleak place.'

And nor can it ever be forgotten amid the mundanity of everyday life, and of ambition, achievement and age. It is that – not a source of pain but of wonder – which I have been taught by my little ghost of ten winters.

# Suggested Reading

Philippe Ariès, *Western Attitudes to Death from the Middle Ages to the Present*, 1976
——*The Hour of our Death*, 1981

Herman Feifel (ed.), *The Meaning of Death*, 1965

Geoffrey Gorer, *Death, Grief and Mourning in Contemporary Britain*, 1965

Robert E. Kavanagh, *Facing Death*, 1974

Elisabeth Kübler-Ross, *On Death and Dying*, 1970

C.S. Lewis , *A Grief Observed*, 1961

Colin Murray Parkes, *Bereavement*, 1975

Lily Pincus, *Death and the Family*, 1976